977772

£10

03116

£50
£5

59773

HIEROGLYPHS
TO
ALPHABETS

HIEROGLYPHS
TO
ALPHABETS

Charles King

FREDERICK MULLER LIMITED · LONDON

First published in Great Britain 1977 by
Frederick Muller Limited, London, NW2 6LE

ISBN 0 584 10134 1

Printed in Great Britain of offset lithography
by Billing & Sons Limited
Guildford, London & Worcester

Contents

List of Illustrations

Introduction

The purpose of this book is to describe the work carried out by archaeologists, Egyptologists and Assyriologists on the ancient hieroglyphic and cuneiform inscriptions and writings which, for centuries, had remained shrouded in mystery. Scholars everywhere became excited when the first efforts in deciphering seemed to be crowned with success, and the ensuing years of arduous labour at length enabled the translations themselves to shed a great deal of light upon the manners, customs and the everyday life of the kings, priests and ordinary people of the past ages.

Making certain marks to convey information must have been one of the first endeavours of civilised man, and the various races managed to develop some system of writing at a very early stage in their history. Ordinary trade and business, not to mention diplomacy, demanded a system of writing for recording decisions and actions taken, together with a system of symbols for numbering.

At various times in their history the countries of the Middle East (the ones we shall be discussing) traded with each other, fought or became allies and then, as now, a command of written and spoken languages was indispensable to the running of a country, and men able to speak and write in several tongues were highly prized. Was it not Napoleon who once said, "A man speaking three languages is three people"?

The actual writing down of words must have posed certain problems for the scribes in the various countries; for instance, what kind of material was available upon which to write? Some had clay, but no material for paper-making, whilst others had only stone, but in each case a special implement had to be invented to make indelible marks upon the surface of the material.

The written language of the ancient Egyptians was highly complex, consisting as it did of more than a thousand little symbols of men, animals, birds, plants, feathers, and articles in everyday use. Then, as happens sometimes today, the government scribe (or civil servant) thought himself a cut above those who worked by the sweat of their brows.

An old story, ancient even when Tutankhamen was on the throne, tells how a scribe, while taking his son to school, compared the superiority of his profession with the various tradesmen and workers they passed on their journey.

"Look, my son, at that blacksmith. It's plain that he'll never attend Court as an ambassador. All day long he kneels working the bellows at his furnace; his skin is like a crocodile, and he stinks like rotten eggs. Look at that stonemason over there splitting that granite block — all day he chips and wrestles with hard stones and rocks, and at the end of the day his arms are worn out and he sleeps all doubled up because of his aching body. Look at Atef the barber just crossing the way; he's shaving people all day from dawn to dusk, hardly daring to sit down to eat his bread. He rushes from house to house in the hope that he'll get there before his rival, and he wears out his arms and fingers just to fill his stomach, like bees eating their own honey. You saw that farmer we passed? He wears the same stinking clothes year in and year out. He can never rest because there is so much to do. He sleeps in the mud with his animals and he's covered with filth like the beasts! Therefore, my son, give all your attention to learning, to the use of the reed brush and your letters, for truly, there is nothing that can compare with it for providing a comfortable life, and if you succeed at school, *it is a gain for eternity.*"

8

Chapter 1

In these pages we shall be discussing several varieties of ancient Middle Eastern scripts dealing, firstly, with the hieroglyphic writing of the ancient Egyptians. However, before doing so, it will be useful and instructive to become acquainted with some basic facts about ancient Egypt and its people.

About 7500 years ago, a race of people migrated from somewhere in Central Asia, and made their laborious way to the Nile Valley by way of Mesopotamia, Arabia, and across the Isthmus of Suez. They were probably a nomadic people, and perhaps great climatic change or warlike neighbours had caused them to leave their Asiatic homeland and move westward. This epic journey must have taken many years — centuries even — but eventually they reached their final home. When they arrived, they found aboriginal races living there, one with a dark skin, the other fair.

We do not know whether they intermarried with the natives, fought with them, or drove them away; it is possible that after a time they all settled down peaceably together, and that the newcomers adopted the customs of their hosts. No traces have come to light of any system of writing from this far-distant period; we do not know if a primitive system of hieroglyphic writing already existed, or whether the 'new Egyptians' brought one with them. One thing is certain, however; Egyptain hieroglyphs began their development at a very early stage in the nation's history. The art of writing belonged to the priests; indeed, the very word 'hieroglyph' means sacred writing (Greek:hieroglyphikon — hieros, sacred; glyphein, to carve).

One of the most remarkable facts about Egyptian hiero-

9

glyphics is how little the characters changed over a period of thousands of years. Why was this? There are several possible answers to this question — priestly influence over the centuries, religious conservatism, or perhaps the Egyptians thought they had arrived at the ultimate in writing systems.

It would perhaps be more accurate to state that the characters *developed* rather than changed; for instance, if one is familiar with the styles of the later dynasties, figures of men, animals and birds carved on slate or stone from the first and second dynasties do not look typically Egyptian. Two such objects spring to mind: the so-called Hunter's palette, and the ceremonial palette of King Narmer. The reader may like to draw his own conclusions from the illustration.

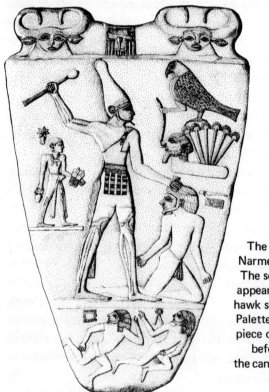

The famous Palette of King Narmer (or Mena). 3500 BC? The somewhat 'un-Egyptain' appearance of the figures and hawk should be observed. The Palette, although an exquisite piece of work, was made long before the period in which the canons for drawing figures, animals and birds were introduced.

What did an ancient Egyptian look like? From drawings, carvings and paintings on monuments, in tombs and on papyri, it appears that he was of slim build, with wide shoulders, and long hands and feet. His eyes were large and dark, his lips full and generous, and his nose short and well shaped. That the paintings are, on the whole, true to life, is confirmed by measurements taken by anthropologists of skulls and bones of mummies; early this century, a theory was put forward which tried to establish the fact that the ancient Egyptian was of Negro origin but this idea was completely refuted by the anthropological evidence.

The inhabitants of Egypt today, especially the Fellahin, the peasants and farmers, greatly resemble their ancestors. Their complexion is dark, they have high cheek-bones, and they have the full lips and broad shoulders so clearly depicted in the tomb paintings.

The Copts (Egyptians having adopted Christianity as their faith) are also descended from the ancient race; while the Fellahin are mainly agriculturists, the Copts are employed as clerks in Government offices, in the postal service and in business houses. It is said that they are quick and efficient at their work but, with a few exceptions, do not rise to the top.

Through the ages, right up to Roman times, the Egyptians were known as "the most religious and superstitious of men", priest-ridden, and obsessed with the after-life. For people of the present day, interested in the past, this is perhaps a fortunate thing since it is a fact that most of our knowledge about ancient Egypt comes from the tombs of kings, noblemen, royal scribes and other notable people of those distant times.

The Egyptians buried their dead in strong tombs, with everything they would need in the life to come such as chariots, weapons, food, wine and beer, reeds and palettes for writing, chairs, couches and chess sets. Accompanying these articles were scores of little figures of human beings which, at the appointed time, would come to life and carry out the necessary

11

everyday tasks for the deceased. Touching on this, I have often wondered whether the householders of today who plant their gardens with gnomes have the same idea in mind!

The excavations of M.J. de Morgan, once Director of the Gizeh Museum in the 1890s, threw light on the customs of the people who inhabited the country before the 'new' Egyptians arrived when, at a place situated a few miles from Abydos, he found a number of pre-dynastic tombs. These were oval pits four to five feet deep in which bodies had been laid on their left side with the legs doubled up and almost touching their chins. The hands were in front of the face. (An example of this type of burial is exhibited in the Egyptian Rooms of the British Museum.) Around the bodies were a number of small pottery vessels filled with burnt bones, and shell bracelets, flints, and objects made in alabaster were also found.

According to de Morgan, these tombs were the graves of neolithic man in Egypt, and some of the bodies seem to have been treated with a preparation of pitch and salt thus making them the oldest examples of mummification known. In 1894-5, Professor Flinders Petrie excavated at a place thirty miles north of Thebes, and found traces of a hitherto unsuspected race who possessed nothing of the Egyptian civilisation. Their graves were square pits usually measuring 6' x 4' x 5' and the body was always laid on its left side in a bent-up position, the head facing to the west.

Two years later, de Morgan excavated some pre-dynastic cemeteries at Nakadah in Upper Egypt. He found tombs belonging to an extremely ancient period, and from his researches he came to the following conclusions:

This race of people had occupied the whole of the Nile Valley, and not just part of it.
Physically, they had nothing in common with the Egyptians; they inhabited the country long before those we call Egyptians, and it was from them that the Egyptians of

dynastic times learned many of their industries, manners and customs.

The excavations showed that the dead were interred in three ways. Firstly with all the bones separated from each other, secondly in the above-mentioned crouching position and, thirdly, with the whole body buried and then burnt in the grave.

All these methods differ greatly from those employed by the Egyptians who, because of their belief that the deceased would come to life again at some future period, always tried to keep the body in as natural a form as possible.

These ancient people may have been members of the tribe of the Tahennu, and pictures in the texts of historical Egyptian kings show them as persons with a light skin, fair hair and blue eyes. If it is correct to conclude that the Egyptians learned much from the original race, may it not be that the Egyptians also obtained the idea of picture-writing from them?

It is because the ancient Egyptians built their palaces, tombs and monuments in durable materials like stone that so much of their history has been bequeathed to us. However, it was not always so, for in the Archaic period temples and palaces, such as they were, were built with wood. As Egypt has never been a wood-producing country, much of their timber had to be imported.

Along with building in wood came brick-making. These were not furnace-baked, but were mixed with straw and sand and put out in the hot sun to dry. The result was quite a superior brick, almost as hard as stone. In wall or tomb construction, various kinds of bondings were used, and for strengthening walls, the principle of buttressing was employed. In some very early tombs, dressed stonework has been found, so even then, metallurgical techniques had been developed sufficiently to produce the tools to cut the stone.

Many people today are vaguely familiar with at least a few proper names of gods, goddesses and kings of Egypt, such as Horus, Osiris, Isis, Rameses, Thothmes, Tutankhamen, and so on. Most of these are not written or pronounced so in hieroglyphic form, which poses the question, why not pronounce the name 'Thothmes' as Te-huti-mes, as it is written? Or again, 'Rameses' as Ra-messu? The answer is that this is the system in general use throughout Europe when using well-known Egyptian proper names. This leads us to the most burning question of all: from what sources have we obtained our knowledge of the history of Egypt? How do we know the names of the scores of dynastic kings?

There are four main sources: The Turin Papyrus, the Tablet of Abydos, the Tablet of Saqqarah, and the Tablet of Karnak. The first, the Turin Papyrus, contained a complete list of kings beginning with the god-kings, going right through until the end of the rule of the Hyksos Asiatic line, about BC 1700. This wonderful document gave the name of each king together with the length of his reign in years, months, and days. When it was found, it was in perfect condition, and it would have been the most valuable archive of all dealing with the oldest part of Egyptian history.

It was packed in a box and sent to Turin. It duly arrived but, horror of horrors, when the box was opened, the papyrus was found to be broken into more than a hundred and fifty fragments. This was a historical tragedy of the first degree, but Champollion was able to place some of the pieces in their chronological order. However, even his gifted efforts failed to provide more than a little information, for the section dealing with the earlier dynasties is of very little value. However, one part of the roll suffered rather less damage than the rest – the section giving the history of the XIIIth and XIVth dynasties is in fairly good condition.

The next source of the king-list is the Tablet of Abydos. This tablet, carved in stone, was discovered in the Temple of Osiris

14

at Abydos during Mariette's excavations there in 1864. Besides the carved list of seventy-five of their ancestors, King Seti and his son are shown honouring their names and memories with incense. The list begins with Mena, the first king of the first dynasty (BC 4400), and ends with Seti I, the father of Rameses II.

Mariette himself discovered the Tablet of Saqqarah in the grave of an important official who lived during the reign of Rameses II; this tablet gives the names of forty-seven kings, and is in accord with the Abydos list, except that it starts with the name of Mer-ba-pen, the sixth king of the first dynasty.

The fourth source, the Tablet of Karnak, was found at that place by Burton; it was drawn up in the days of Thothmes III, and contains the names of sixty-one kings. Unfortunately, these are not arranged in the correct order, but the information is of great value because it records the names of some of the kings from the XIIIth to the XVIIth dynasties. It also gives in more detail the names and reigns of the rulers of the XIth dynasty than any other list.

There is one more source of Egyptian history — the fragmentary remains of a black basalt slab called the Palermo Stone. Only five small pieces remain to us, and no one knows where to look for the greater part which, when whole, may have measured about seven feet by two. The largest piece is deposited in the Museum at Palermo, hence its name. It is thought that the slab may have contained the names of every king of the Archaic Period, the years of their reigns and some of the most important events that took place during the period. This, like the ill-fated Turin Papyrus, was another tragedy for archaeological research. It is to be hoped that archaeological patience will one day be rewarded by the discovery of a complete and reliable document yielding information from the Archaic Period.

How did the dynastic system in Egypt come into being? It is due to the work of a priest and scribe named Manetho (living in BC 271); his Egyptian name was Meri-en-Tehuti, meaning beloved of Thoth, and he was commissioned to write a history of Egypt by Ptolemy II Philadelphus. Although the original work is lost, versions of his lists of Egyptian kings have been preserved in the works of Eusebius and Africanus.

It is not known why Manetho divided up the thirty dynasties into three main sections, but they are presented to us as the Ist to XIth, the XIIth to XIXth and the XXth to XXXth which correspond roughly with the Old Kingdom, the Middle Kingdom and the New Kingdom. That the Egyptians themselves did not divide their royal reigns into dynasties is proved by the Tablets of Abydos and Saqqarah.

Other sources of history can be obtained from inscriptions carved upon the walls of temples, obelisks and buildings, as well as from the stelae and papyri upon which Egyptian kings caused records of their principal victories and the lands they conquered to be drawn up; many of these details are dated, and throw much welcome light on the nation's history. Lists of tribute from conquered peoples are sometimes given, and from these we learn the nature of the various countries' products.

Another fascinating find from the past were 310 tablets inscribed in cuneiform characters unearthed in 1887 at Tell el-Amarna. They are letters written on clay tablets in the strange wedge-shaped characters used by the Assyrians and Babylonians, (Latin:- cuneus, a wedge) and were sent by the kings of Babylon to King Amenophis III and to his son Akhenaten (or Amenophis IV).

The monuments and writings of the Egyptians excited great curiosity among the Greeks and Romans, and some of their scholars were sufficiently keen to do more than stare and wonder — men like Hecataeus of Miletus, who went to Egypt between BC 513-501. From him, through Herodotus, we gained much knowledge about the Egyptians and their customs. Herodotus, a true seeker after truth, was often misinformed (or had his leg pulled unmercifully) by people he met and who showed him around. His chapters dealing with the Egyptians are always entertaining, especially the second 'book' called *Euterpe* (The History of Herodotus, Trans. George Rawlinson, Dent).

Hellanitis (BC 470-393) in his work *Aigyptiaka* showed that he was successful in translating many of the Egyptian characters. Other writers such as Democritus and Diodorus were keen Egyptologists; they too were among the first pioneers in deciphering the hieroglyphs. The work of another scholar, Clement of Alexandria (191-220 AD) was of great value to Champollion, a brilliant young Frenchman of the nineteenth century.

Chapter 2

Egypt has always been a land of mystery and magic, and for centuries archaeologists, lovers of history and the merely curious, have gazed wonderingly upon the inscriptions cut into stone slabs and columns and have racked their brains trying to establish a clue to the strange hieroglyphs written on sheets of papyrus, or the neat wedge-shaped markings on clay cylinders.

In order to express their ideas in permanent form, the Egyptians used over a thousand pictorial signs, usually beautifully drawn or carved and from earliest times (more than six thousand years ago) until about BC100, these symbols were employed without interruption, especially by the priests. Many state documents, royal decrees, as well as the sacred books were written in hieroglyphs, but at a fairly early, although as yet unascertained date, a modified cursive form known as Hieratic came into use.

The salient characteristics remained, but many of the signs were abbreviated, and this form of writing was used by scribes and priests in copying religious and literary works. Hieratic script was rarely used upon statues, tombs, coffins or temples because these situations demanded the highest form of the time-honoured hieroglyphs.

A third form of writing came into being which was used for business and social purposes; this is known as Demotic, and is really a kind of 'shorthand'. It has little in common with the attractive hieroglyphs. (Greek:demotikos, the writing of the people.)

Naturally, any scribe worth his salt could write in all three forms, but the characters in which he wrote depended on the

18

job in hand. Chapters from the Book of the Dead were usually written in hieroglyphs or hieratic, and only rarely in demotic.

Hieratic, the abbreviated form of picture-writing, had to come. A priest, having the laborious work of copying thousands of characters, or a scribe taking dictation, would naturally tend to gloss over and 'streamline' the figures; as long as other people could read it easily and the work looked neat and tidy, all was well and, as a result, at some distant date the hieratic form came to be accepted.

The Greeks are recorded as having expressed their debt and admiration to the Egyptians, especially for their invention of paper-making. The plant from which they made their papyri once grew plentifully in large areas of the Delta, the so-called papyrus swamps. There are a few specimens of this plant (Cyperus papyrus) in the Cairo Botanical Gardens but the reeds used by the scribes as writing brushes (Juncus maritimus) still grow in the salt marshes.

The word for 'papyrus' was written ⟨hieroglyphs⟩ (thuf) or ⟨hieroglyphs⟩ (thufi); and in Coptic, ⲭⲟⲟⲩϥ (ghoof). It was a most useful plant; some authorities have maintained that the large cabbage-like leaves could be cooked and eaten, while the tough roots served as firewood, and from the parts not used for paper-making, strong ropes were made and baskets and mats were woven. The long thick stalks were even used for making light boats and in many tomb paintings, the deceased is often shown hunting from a papyrus boat made by lashing the stalks together and reinforcing them with wood. There was a tradition that a man would be perfectly safe from attack by crocodiles in a papyrus boat.

The Egyptians were fortunate in the use they made of the products of the papyrus swamps; while the Babylonians and Assyrians were scratching their letters on heavy clay tablets, paper-making was already an advanced art in Egypt. But it must be admitted that the Assyrian cuneiform characters were the ideal type of markings for working on new clay, and that this material took the impression of the writing tool very well. On the other hand, prepared papyrus was the ideal material upon which to inscribe hieroglyphs, for which clay tablets would have been most unsuitable.

So which, in history, came first, the tool or the medium? I am inclined to think the former. After all, the pen or brush is really but an extension of man's forefinger when he made his first marks in the sand or mud.

In Egypt, several qualities and various widths of papyrus paper were produced for different uses. The stalk of the plant grew to a height of between fourteen and twenty feet, was triangular in section, and about six inches in diameter at its thickest part. Firstly, the outer rind was removed, and a flat needle or spatula was used to divide the stalk into thin layers which were then laid side by side on a flat table. The layers were painted with a solution of gum, and another series of strips were then laid crosswise upon them. With great care, the length was beaten with a wooden mallet, pressed down and, finally, the surface was polished with a smooth flat stone. When newly made the papyrus rolls were of an off-white colour but, through the ages, they tended to darken. This was due to natural causes, such as the effects of soil; some papyri are of a warm light-brown colour, while others are very dark indeed.

Workshops existed all over Egypt where papyrus rolls were turned out in quantity, but it was mainly in the regions where the plant grew that production was highest. A complete roll consisted of twenty sheets of about fifteen inches in length, that is to say, about twenty-five feet. An overlap of about a quarter of an inch was allowed for joining one sheet to another, and they were stuck down with gum, starch paste, or white of egg.

Inside the roll, the side used for writing upon, the fibres ran horizontally, and a papyrus was always rolled — never folded. It is not known when this material was first used for paper-making; the earliest papyrus extant with written inscriptions consists mainly of fragments; they are from books from the Funerary Temple of King Nefer-ka-ari-Ra ⊙ | 🝙 of the Vth dynasty (BC 3366).

Although the average length of a roll of papyrus was twenty-five feet, there were exceptions such as the Great Papyrus of Rameses III which is 135 feet long and 16½ inches wide. Similarly a copy of the Book of the Dead made for a princess of the XXIst dynasty is 123 feet long and 18 inches in width. This papyrus is unusual in that it is composed of three layers of papyrus fibres; it is written mainly in hieratic script and contains 2,600 lines of text.

Papyrus used for ordinary literary work and documents came in smaller sizes ranging in length from ten to twenty feet and in the region of nine inches in width. Papyrus was expensive, and it was never wasted; a sheet would sometimes be used again if the previous writing could be erased.

The word for scroll or book was ⩰?| (chama), and in Coptic, Ⲭ ⲟ ⲱ ⲓ (ghomi). When not in use, a roll was carefully rolled up, tied with a cord and put in a safe place. Before important documents were sent out a seal of mud or wax, bearing an impression from a scarab ring, would be laid on the knot.

For writing, the scribe used selected reeds; the tip was sliced at an angle, and chewed until it acted like a small brush. These reeds were about ten inches long and an eighth of an inch thick. The sign for the writing reed was ⌂ 🝙 (gash); Coptic, ⲕ ⲁ ⲱ (kash). The palette, made of wood or perhaps a piece of worked slate, was about a foot long and contained two round hollows to take the cakes of black and red paint. Some of them had a slot for reeds.

The scribe usually wrote sitting cross-legged, but he would sometimes stand. When his 'brush' was going well, he could make eight or nine signs with one dip of the reed.

21

If he made a mistake he either licked away the error or used the corner of a damp rag. When he had a long document to write or copy he would sit cross-legged with the roll of papyrus resting upon his stretched tight kilt. He would start from the right-hand side, leaving a wide margin between the vertical edge and the first line of script.

Page numbering was uncommon, but this was done in the case of the famous Ebers Papyrus, a work dealing with medical matters. Direction of writing was from the top of the page to the bottom; this has certain disadvantages in that the previous line can be easily smudged. The scribes of Babylon and China also wrote in the vertical direction, but it was not unknown for them to use the horizontal occasionally. It was not until the XIIth dynasty (about BC 2466) that the shift from vertical to horizontal writing became usual in Egypt.

Much of the literature that has come down to us is of a religious character, and perhaps the most important is the collection of chapters known as the Book of the Dead (in the ancient tongue, per em hru, 'Coming forth by day'). These chapters contain prayers, incantations and addresses to the gods from whom the deceased hoped to be granted everlasting life. The origin of the chapters is of great antiquity, so much so, in fact, that some of the material was obscure even to the priests of later times.

Many copies are illustrated with vignettes in colour, which go along with the text. In ancient Egypt, it was considered to be most unsafe to be buried without a few chapters from this work. These and certain other magical papyri practically guaranteed that the deceased would reach the Elysian Fields and live for ever, provided that all the injunctions were carried out, and that he knew the names of all the gods who would pass him through.

Scribes and people of rank had beautiful copies prepared and buried with them, but ordinary folk purchased cheaper versions from 'booksellers'. These merchants sold other funerary accessories, such as the little ushabti figures, charms, amulets and spells, and had stocks of chapters of the Book of the Dead in various qualities, plain, or with coloured illustrations.

Chapters bought from stock have been found; they were detected as such because in many cases the scribes left large blank spaces in the first column which has been filled in by another hand in cursive script awkwardly squeezed in, or in very bad writing. These additions would consist of the names and title of the deceased.

The Egyptian book in the form of a roll underwent few changes for about thirty centuries; the Egyptians were not the only people who thought they had discovered the perfect way to put down their thoughts − China and Japan, too, had their long scrolls.

Three thousand years of Egyptian civilisation passed before the roll of papyrus was replaced by a new form, the codex − a series of tablets tied together by cords passed through holes on one of their vertical sides.

Besides papyrus, other materials were used for writing upon, such as fine skin, thin slabs of white limestone, and squares of wood painted over with a kind of gesso; these were quite suitable and far cheaper than papyrus paper. Schoolboys and students wrote upon limestone slabs, while a scribe in his professional capacity would use the gessoed wood for roughing out complicated documents before producing the finished work on papyrus.

The great Egyptian god Thoth (Tehuti) is the god of learning and it is he who is credited with having invented the art of writing. Indeed, the hieroglyphic characters were known to the Egyptians as "the writing of the words of the god".

The inks used by the scribes were made of lamp-black mixed with gum and water; they were not waterproof like our own Indian inks and would readily smear. Indelible inks were probably made from a mixture of wine in which galls had been soaked, while the beautiful blues and greens used in illustrating the best quality books came from preparations of copper. Reds were obtained from red ochre.

Chapter 3

The interest of the Greeks and Romans in Egyptian antiquities has been mentioned; they were also vastly intrigued by the hieroglyphs, and scholars like Hellanitis and Clement had some success in deciphering the strange characters. Their results were more fruitful than the efforts of the scholars of the sixteenth to eighteenth centuries, among them one Athanasius Kircher, who pretended to have found the key to the inscriptions and to have translated them.

In the opinion of modern scholars, however, his work is regarded as a farrago of nonsense. In 1774, another enthusiast, Joseph de Guignes, produced a treatise in which he tried to prove that Egyptian characters were to be found in Chinese, and that the Chinese nation was merely an Egyptian colony.

One scholar who contributed something of value to Egyptology was Zoega; in 1797 he became convinced that the hieroglyphs were letters, and that the oval cartouches contained the names of kings. At about this time, men of letters were in a high state of excitement and enthusiasm, and the wildest ideas about the hieroglyphs were being proposed by people who should have known better.

In a way, they cannot be blamed for their misplaced enthusiasm for, as we have noted, even writers and scholars living five hundred years before the birth of Christ were dazzled by the mystery of Egypt and her hieroglyphs.

With the work of Young and Champollion, however, we are on firm ground; they have the distinction of being the true discoverers of the correct method of deciphering the inscriptions.

The conquest of Egypt by the Greeks sounded the death knell of the ancient Egyptian language. The subject Egyptians were not prohibited from making use of their native tongue, but little by little the best positions in the government service were taken over by Greeks. Meanwhile, King Ptolemy I succeeded in attracting to Alexandria the finest Greek scholars of the day; the great Alexandrian Library and Museum were founded and well endowed for the support and benefit of the most eminent Greek philosophers and literati. Ptolemy's firm aim was to make the learning and language of his Greeks the dominant force in Egypt.

Although Ptolemy II Philadelphus ordered Manetho to write a history of Egypt together with an account of the ancient religion, he was steadily working to drive the native people into obscurity. He even suppressed many of the ancient foundations including the priest-college at Heliopolis.

Gradually, the noble language and "the writing of the words of the god" faded from men's minds. Two hundred years or so after the Christian era had begun, Egyptians who had embraced the faith, the followers and disciples of St Mark, had no choice but to use the Greek alphabet to write down the Egyptian (Coptic) translations of the Old and New Testaments. Thus, except for a few scattered pockets of learning, knowledge of hieroglyphic writing practically died out and, within a century or so, no one could be found who could understand a word of it.

THE ROSETTA STONE

The story of the discovery of this slab of black basalt and the decipherment of its inscriptions reads like a romance.

Long before the end of Roman rule in Egypt, the sacred hieroglyphic writing had become redundant, even the quickly-written demotic's days were numbered; Coptic, which is Egyptian written in Greek, had taken their place, but only among the Christian priests. Now was the age of Greek and

Latin, and to the passer-by, the beautiful hieroglyphics inscribed upon columns and monuments had become meaningless symbols.

The might of Egypt with its great gods and kings "whose names liveth forever" was eclipsed by more vigorous and enterprising people; nevertheless, through the centuries, scholarly visitors to Egypt continued to be intrigued and fascinated by the carved inscriptions of men, animals, birds and mysterious objects cut deeply into stone.

Up to the discovery of the Rosetta Stone which provided the key to Egyptian hieroglyphics, there were quite a number of unscrupulous persons who, for reasons of profit or acquisition of fame to which they were not entitled, pretended to have discovered the meaning of the strange symbols and published so-called translations. Needless to say, their 'translations' were nonsense; many of these people were of the opinion that the inscriptions were of a biblical nature, or even Psalms from the Old Testament.

In the seventeenth and eighteenth centuries, there were several genuine attempts by scholars to interpret the meanings of the hieroglyphs, but their work came to nothing, because their researches were not founded upon the right lines, and they lacked knowledge of the work done by the Greeks.

The Rosetta Stone, which stands at the southern end of the Egyptian Gallery of the British Museum, was found at a spot near the town of Rashid, or Rosetta as it is more commonly known.

At the time, in 1799, the French were in command of Egypt, and a French officer of Engineers called Boussard was the discoverer of the famous relic. One account says the stone was lying on the ground when found; according to another, it was built into an old wall which the French officers were about to demolish.

Boussard, noticing the three groups of inscriptions, reported the discovery to his general, who ordered him to have it brought to his house in Alexandria, and there it remained for two years.

Napoleon Bonaparte, having heard about the stone and its inscriptions, ordered it to be taken to Cairo and deposited in the Institut National. Napoleon himself and the group of learned men he had brought with him on the expedition to Egypt showed the greatest interest in it, and the Emperor ordered a number of copies to be taken from the surface of the stone and sent to scholars in all the capitals of Europe.

Two lithographers from Paris arrived in Cairo to carry out this task; their method was to cover the surface of the stone with printer's ink, lay upon it a sheet of suitable paper, then roll it with rubber rollers to obtain a good impression.

Meanwhile, Napoleon's fortunes had begun to wane, and in 1801 a Treaty of Capitulation was drawn up. Among its various Articles, the Rosetta Stone and many other important and valuable Egyptian antiquities were surrendered to the British. The bulk of the objects were sent by naval vessels at once to England, but the Rosetta Stone left Egypt some time later in the year.

After the French printers had carried out their work the stone was returned to the general's house but, later that year, it was claimed by Major-General Turner. He had some difficulty in obtaining possession of it, as the Frenchman regarded it as his own property. It was acquired, however, and on arrival at Portsmouth was taken to London where it was eagerly examined by oriental and Greek scholars. Several plaster casts made from it were presented to the four main British universities. Copies of the Greek text on the stone were sent to all the universities, libraries and academies in Europe.

Description of the Stone

It is a large slab of black basalt, eleven inches thick, with the top left, top right, and the right-hand bottom corners missing. It was certainly somewhat larger in its original state, and the top was most probably rounded. This space may have borne a design in relief of the winged disc of Horus bearing the two sacred ser-

The Rosetta Stone inscribed in Greek, Egyptian hieroglyphic and demotic characters.

pents, and below this design may have figured the king with his queen accompanied by several gods.

The stone in its present state measures three feet nine inches in length, and two feet four and a half inches in width, and it is thought that when it was complete, it could have been over five feet long. The relevant part of this description concerns the inscriptions, which are in two languages, that is to say, in Egyptian and Greek. The top section is engraved in Egyptian hieroglyphics; below this comes the version in demotic characters, while at the bottom we see the Greek.

The hieroglyphic section consists of only fourteen lines and these correspond to the last twenty-eight lines of Greek. There are thirty-two lines of demotic text, the first fourteen unfortunately being incomplete at the beginnings.

The Greek inscription takes up fifty-four lines, and about twenty-six of these are imperfect or missing at the ends. There is also a hole in the middle and to the right of the Greek section.

We are fortunate in that the missing hieroglyphs at both the top left and right of the slab are not lost to us; a stele found at Damanhur in 1898 contained the missing lines. In addition, there is a complete text cut on the walls of a temple at Philae, so that the complete set of inscriptions, both in Egyptian and Greek, are known to us.

Who was it that ordered the Rosetta Stone to be made, and what is the meaning of the inscriptions carved upon it?

Round about the year BC 198, the land of Egypt must have been suffering from a period of great food shortage, possibly due to crop failure on a large scale. An epidemic of cattle disease may have run riot through the country. We do not know what happened, but something was done, strong and vigorous action was taken to put the troubles to rights. The Priesthood wished to show its gratitude to the young king; the priests at Memphis held a General Council, and the Rosetta Stone is a copy of the Decree they passed at the meeting.

This stated that the Priesthood at Memphis was grateful to

Ptolemy V Epiphanes, King of Egypt, for the great irrigation works he caused to be carried out to the benefit of the country; for the remission of taxes due from the hard-pressed people and for the revenues he conferred upon the Priesthood for the up-keep of the temples. Among other benefits were gifts of money and corn to the temples; abolition of the press-gang for sailors; forgiveness of rebels, who were now permitted to return to Egypt and live in peace; an amnesty for long-term prisoners; reduction of the tax on corn lands and, finally, restoration and rebuilding of ruined temples and shrines.

The priests, for their part, agreed to increase the ceremonial observances of honour to Ptolemy, "the ever-living", in the temples. It was also ordered that a statue of the king should be set up in every temple in Egypt; that a gilded wooden statue should be placed in every temple, and as an additional honour to His Majesty, it was arranged that a copy of the Decree inscribed on a stone stele in hieroglyphics, demotic and Greek, should be set up in each of the first, second and third grade temples.

It was also decided to distinguish the shrine of the 'Saviour of Egypt' by means of ten double crowns of gold, and to make the anniversaries of his birthday and coronation day festival days for ever. This, in brief, is the meaning of the inscriptions on the Rosetta Stone.

Tremendous interest in the inscriptions was aroused among scholars everywhere, and each in his own way set to work at once upon the difficult task of deciphering the hieroglyphics and trying to match them with the Greek section. Although Egyptian was a dead language, Greek was not, and very soon, a translation of the Greek text was made by the Reverend Stephen Weston, who communicated his results to the members of the Society of Antiquaries in London in April 1802.

Hot upon its heels came a translation of the Greek text in French, but deciphering the Egyptian characters was another matter. In the same year, Akerblad and Silvestre de Sacy concentrated their minds upon the demotic inscriptions, and published an alphabet of the characters, with a note about the 'cartouches', the ovals in the hieroglyphic text, containing royal names.

Akerblad did not receive full credit for his studies, which were valuable and on the right track; today, however, the work he did is fully appreciated by scholars.

In 1818, Dr Thomas Young published his 'Supposed Enchorial Alphabet', and fourteen of the characters are identical with those of poor Akerblad, who once again received no credit. Young was the first man to see that there was a phonetic principle involved in the reading of the hieroglyphics, and he was able to make translations of the three inscriptions, the results of his efforts being published in 1821. Thomas Young was born of Quaker parents at Milverton in Somerset on the 13th June, 1773. By all accounts he had a great aptitude for languages; it is said that by the time he was fourteen years of age he was conversant in Greek, Latin, French, Italian, Hebrew, Persian and Arabic. By profession he was a physician, and had many other scientific interests. He died in 1829.

Jean François Champollion le Jeune, born at Figeac in France in 1796, was a brilliant scholar and in 1822 published his own translation of the inscriptions. The earlier work of Dr Young was of considerable help to the young archaeologist, but it contained many errors. Champollion deciphered the hieroglyphic forms of the names and titles of most of the Roman emperors; created a system of grammar, and founded the system upon which later Egyptologists were to rely.

He attacked his task with scientific zeal, and was the better armed for the work by his great knowledge of Coptic, an advantage which Young lacked.

Champollion was educated at Grenoble, and later in Paris, where he devoted much time to the study of the Coptic language. Charles X commissioned him to visit all the important collections of Egyptian antiquities in Europe, and on his return he was appointed Director of the Louvre. In 1828 he was sent on a scientific expedition to Egypt, and was afterwards made Professor of Egyptian Studies at the Collège de France.

So hard did he work, and so ardently did his spirit burn in the cause, that his body could not stand the strain. He fell ill, and at the early age of forty-two he died. His brother carried on the good work after his death, and looked after his interests, but death had extinguished the vital spark of Champollion the younger; the brother's work was of considerable value, but it lacked the drive and brilliance of the younger man.

Another outstanding worker in this field was Mr J.W. Bankes, who discovered a red granite obelisk on the Island of Philae in 1815, and had it brought at his own expense to England. Each side of the obelisk bears a column of hieroglyphics, and the pedestal is inscribed with twenty-four lines of Greek.

Mr Bankes deciphered the name of Kleopatra from the hieroglyphic inscription, while Champollion published an account of the obelisk in the *Revue Encyclopédique*, wherein he discussed the Greek and Egyptian inscriptions carved upon it.

The names of the Englishman Dr Samuel Birch, the German Dr Lepsius, and the Italians Rosellini and Salvolini should also be remembered as earnest pioneers in the field of hieroglyphic cipherment.

Earlier in the text an indication was given of how little the hieroglyphic signs appeared to change over the thousands of years they were in use, but this statement prompts the rather obvious question, changed from what? At what period in Egyptian history was some sort of sign alphabet invented?

Despite the meticulous searches of the world's archaeologists among the dusty tombs of the Archaic period, little has come to light which pre-dates the reign of King Mena (or Narmer; many scholars are of the opinion that Mena and Narmer were the same person). In Mena's time (circa 3,000 BC) the hieroglyphic signs were already conventionalised; a cursive script was already in use together with a system of numerical signs. But there came a time when all the little drawings became standardised; at some period after Mena, a complete phonetic system of writing developed. Before this, however, the inscriptions on seals, labels and other relics which have been unearthed gave great difficulties to the decipherers and, even now, many of the inscriptions defy interpretation.

When the system of writing became fully developed it remained virtually unchanged until the eclipse of Egyptian writing by the Greek.

It is fascinating to contemplate some great conference of royal scribes living in the times of the kings of the first dynasty, sitting in session for many months, years even, shaping the written language, composing the 'alphabet', once and for all time allotting sounds and meanings to thousands of little picture-symbols that would represent man, woman and child in dozens of meaningful attitudes; every animal, bird, fish, insect, tree and plant; every kind of rock and stone, temples and their various parts, ships, boats — the list is endless.

The great task would include the formulation and refining of the national Egyptian grammar with its verbs, adjectives, pronouns and so on, and at a guess, a great dictionary was composed which would be copied in great numbers by armies of scribes.

In time, no doubt, every temple, school and government office would have a copy in its possession, while every scribe worth the name would have as part of his general equipment an abridged version of the standard dictionary.

So far, unfortunately, the excavator's pick has failed to bring to light any examples of any kind of dictionary; this is not surprising, since papyrus is not known for its indestructibility.

We now arrive at the stage where some concrete examples of

34

the hieroglyphics and their meanings can be discussed. The Egyptians used over two thousand characters or pictographs, either singly or in combination, but the space allowed here will only enable us to deal with a few of them.

When the early would-be decipherers were confronted with a slab of stone containing a column of hieroglyphs, they were also confronted with a real mystery — it was even worse when the inscription ran horizontally; at which end did one begin? There are four ways in which to write Egyptian hieroglyphics, and in reading them, the point to remember is to read them from the end they face, that is, if the men, birds and animals are looking to the left, one reads from left to right. Examples are given of this later on.

What was the method used by Champollion and Bankes to solve the puzzle of the hieroglyphs? To begin with, it was assumed that the oval shapes, called cartouches, contained royal names. 'Cartouche' is a word meaning cartridge. The Rosetta Stone contained a cartouche which was repeated five times, all having the same characters inscribed in them and which were assumed to form the name Ptolemy, since it could be seen from the Greek text that a Ptolemy was mentioned in it. It was thought, reasonably enough, that if the ovals really did contain Ptolemy's name, the little signs would have the sound-values of the Greek letters.

On Bankes's red granite obelisk, the inscriptions are in Greek and Egyptian; in the Greek, two royal names appear, Ptolemy, and Kleopatra, while in the Egyptian portion there are two cartouches lying close together and containing neatly arranged symbols.

Again, it was considered that the enclosed hieroglyphs might possess the identical sound-values with the two names, and when they were carefully copied down and compared with the oval on the Rosetta Stone, it was seen that one of the cartouches from the obelisk was almost the same as that in the cartouche on the Stone.

35

Slowly and painfully the work of deciphering proceeded. Young had previously solved the name of Ptolemy on the Stone as well as that of Berenice from another inscription elsewhere. From the Philae obelisk, Bankes had successfully deciphered the name of Kleopatra; both in Ptolemy and Kleopatra some of the letters are repeated, that is, P T O L.

Shown here are the cartouches containing Ptolemy's name from A, the Rosetta Stone, and B, the Philae obelisk:

Upon examination, the Philae oval will be seen to possess an extra sign 𝒪, and a different arrangement at the end of the group.

This is the name of Kleopatra as it appears on the Philae obelisk: and so that we can make our comparison in order to gain some letters we give the symbols for Ptolemy and Kleopatra in an extended form and numbered, so:

It will be seen at once that A1 and B5 are the same, and should represent the letter P. Next, A4 and B2 are also identical, and from their position it was judged that this should make an L.

If this is correct, and L being the second letter in the word Kleopatra, B1 must represent the letter K or C.

The name Kleopatra has a double vowel between the L and P, and amidst the line of symbols there are two hieroglyphs 𝄃 and 𝒪, so we will call 𝄃 = E and 𝒪 = O. But what about the

36

sign ⌒ B7?

Sometimes, Egyptian spelling varies, and frequently ⌒ is given the same value as △, which is T. As there is a 'T' sound in Kleopatra, we can assume that this is the case here.

The two 'A' sounds in Kleopatra are identified by the eagle B6 and B9. Let us see the result:

KLEOPAT⌒A ○

Only one sign remains in line B, and that is ⌒, and it is obvious that this has the value of R.

Regarding the last two symbols in line B, these always occur at the ends of cartouches containing names of goddesses or queens of Egypt. And now the name of Kleopatra stands deciphered. How does this help us to solve the name of Ptolemy? Let us apply the letters we have gained from Kleopatra to the cartouche of Ptolemy;

PTOL ⌒ 𓏲𓏲𓏭𓆳𓂝 T ⌒ PT 𓏏 ⊏⊐

This name is obviously Ptolemy (or the Greek Ptolemaios), but there are as yet several unfamiliar hieroglyphs to be deciphered. The Egyptian scribes, as we have noted, sometimes varied their spelling of royal names, especially if they were foreign ones, but the usual way to write Ptolemaios was:

□𓂋𓆳 𓏲𓏲𓏭 the last sign representing an 'S'. It only remains to clarify ⌒ and 𓏲𓏲, and their position in the name seem to indicate values of M and EE (or AI) respectively.

What about the last group of hieroglyphics, 𓆳𓆰𓂝□𓏏 ⊏⊐? Now we are in the secret, it all seems so easy, but it caused the early decipherers, and even Champollion himself quite a few headaches. Much of the work of deciphering was pure guesswork and deduction, like working on a super crossword puzzle. Champollion's successes were due to his own fiery genius combined with the knowledge gained in his deep studies of the old Coptic language, and regarding this, he knew that the word for 'life' or 'living' was ānkh or ōnkh, and that it was represented

37

by the first sign ☥.

He deduced that the next group of symbols meant 'ever'; in Coptic, one of the ancient words for ever or eternity was 'djet'. As we know the little ⌓-shaped symbol is T, then clearly ≈ must have the sound of 'tch'.

The sign ⟲ is a determinative and has no sound. So now we have ☥ ≈ as meaning, 'living for ever'.

The last four symbols were found to include the name of the god Ptah; we know that ⊡ = PT, so § must make some kind of H sound, either hard or soft.

The fourth and remaining symbol ⊞, Champollion deduced, had the value of 'mer'; he was aided by his knowledge of the Coptic word for 'to love', which is mere = ⲙⲉⲡⲉ. The result is the title, 'Beloved of Ptah'.

If we return a moment to the cartouche of Ptolemy from the Rosetta Stone, it will be seen that the last group was given as ⤬ ⸦⸧, and this Champollion found, gave the equivalent value of ⊞, mere, 'beloved', where ⤬ = M and ⸦⸧ = EE.

Caesar or Kaiser as the title of the Roman emperors is familiar to most people; written in hieroglyphics it appears like this:

⌣ ⸦⸧ ⎰ ⌢ ⎯ KAISRS

This gives us two new characters, No 1 and No 5, but the decipherers found that No 1 = K, was sometimes used to begin the name of Kleopatra, while ⎯ is merely a variant of ⎰ = S.

In order to add a few more letters to our store, let us consider the hieroglyphs contained in the following cartouches:

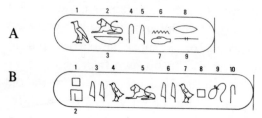

Let us consider cartouche A first. Which of the symbols are we familiar with, and which ones are new to us? 1, 2, 3, 4, 5, 8 and 9 we have met with already; only 6 and 7 are new. Once again we will string them out in a mixed line of Roman letters and hieroglyphics.

ALKSA ᗰᗰᗰ ᑕ RS

It seems to us, as it seemed to Champollion, that the name must be Alexandros, so 6 and 7 must represent the sounds for N and D.

In cartouche B, Nos 2, 4 and 7 are new.

P ▢ EE ⟩ LEE ⟩ POS

No 2 could represent an enclosure, while 4 and 7 is a chick. Although there is an 'F' sound in hieroglyphic form, the scribes apparently chose in this instance to use the Greek PH for the first letter of this name. Regarding the chick sign, I have seen Ptolemy spelled 'Ptulmis' = ▢ ⟩ ᗌ ❨❨❩, so from this, we can give the chick the sound-value of U. We now obtain the Greek name of PHIULIUPOS = Philip.

Chapter 4

Before making any further attempts to decipher royal names and titles, it would be instructive to give the reader the complete Egyptian alphabet together with the alphabet of the Copts. This will be seen to provide a link in sound-values, because the old sounds still live to a certain extent today in the Coptic tongue.

Egyptian words were composed mainly of consonants; hieroglyphic writing ignored or omitted vowel sounds. For instance, there is not, as far as we know, any sound of 'e' (as in egg), but for the sake of convenience, Egyptologists use the 'e' sound in words like 〔⸗ 'amen' (hidden) and ⊖ 'chet' (thing).

The alphabetical signs are composed of both familiar and unfamiliar objects; the meaning of which are depicted later, where known.

THE EGYPTIAN HIEROGLYPHIC ALPHABET

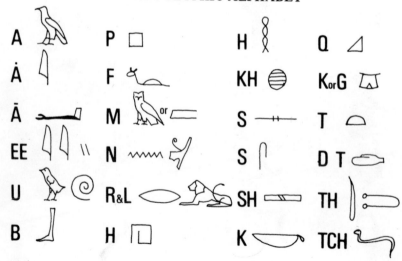

Egyptologists are convinced that these values are accurate, and
this is supported, when they occur in Coptic words, by the
sounds in the Coptic alphabet:

COPTIC ALPHABET

ⲁ	a	ⲓ	i	ⲣ	r	ⲱ	sh
Ⲃ	b	Ⲕ	k	Ⲥ	s	ϥ	f
Ⲅ	g	ⲗ	l	Ⲧ	t	ϧ	x ch
Ⲇ	d	ⲙ	m	ⲩ	y	ϩ	h̲
Ⲉ	e	Ⲛ	n	Ⲫ	ph	Ⲭ	g
Ⲍ	z	Ⲝ	ks x	Ⲭ	ch	ϭ	ch
Ⲏ	ê	Ⲟ	o	Ⲯ	ps	ϯ	ti
Ⲑ	th	Ⲡ	p	ⲱ	ô		

It should be borne in mind that the Copts, the Egyptians who embraced Christianity, did not write the Scriptures in demotic, but used the Greek alphabet. There were, however, certain sounds in Egyptian for which the Greeks did not have letters, so the Copts devised six signs based upon the old hieroglyphs and added them to their Coptic alphabet. These are the signs, together with their sound values:

ⲱ ϥ ⳉ ⳁ ϭ ⳋ

sh   f   x   ẖ   ch   g

Having constructed such a beautiful but difficult and complicated script, how did the Egyptians make the true meanings of their words known? Even important scribes were known to have made mistakes on occasions; in several papyri and on the walls of tombs, Egyptologists have noted spelling mistakes, words left out, and wrong signs used.

Firstly, hieroglyphics were used in two ways: ideographically and phonetically. In the first, a word was rendered from a standardised pictograph, such as 〰 'mu' for water, but phonetically this was rendered as 🦉 m+u. Another example is ⬭ 'per', house; this can be written as ⬭. Again, ⌒ 'semt', mountains or foreign lands could be expressed as ⌒.

The ideographic system may be older than the phonetic; the latter system however made life easier for the scribes.

The phonetic signs are (1) alphabetical, such as ⌒K, ⌡ B or (2), they are syllabic as in the following examples, 'nefer', meaning 'good' or 'joy': ⌡. This sign can be written in several ways: ⌡; ⌡; or ⌡. We can obtain the Egyptian name of Sneferu by the addition of the S sign at the beginning

42

SOME SOUNDS HAVE MORE THAN ONE SIGN

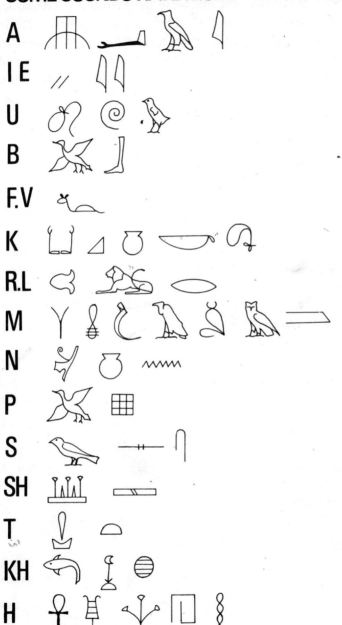

A

I E

U

B

F.V

K

R.L

M

N

P

S

SH

T

KH

H

and the U sign at the end: ⌐〜⸙𝄐

Now to make sure a word was really understood, the use of determinatives came into being at some period, as yet unknown. Here is one example, added to the symbols for 'mau', cat: 𓏏𓏭𓃠 the standard sign for a cat was placed after this word, and this ensured clarity.

Two more examples of the use of determinatives, 'renpit' 𓈖𓇋𓆸𓏥 flowers; here we have a branch in bud, a spray of flowers, and the three vertical strokes indicating the plural. The second example is 'hememu', mankind: 𓏺𓀀𓅓𓀀𓏥. One of the problems facing the early decipherers was to discover from which end the words began. There are four ways in which to read and write Egyptian hieroglyphics, and the important thing to remember is to read them in the opposite way they face. For instance, let us take a short sentence from The Tale of Two Brothers, "He set his load upon the ground". When the characters look to the left

you read them from left to right. In the following example, you read from right to left.

Sometimes the characters are written in vertical columns. If the animals and birds look to the left, you would read them from left to right working downwards.

The fourth way is to reverse these columns and read the signs right to left.

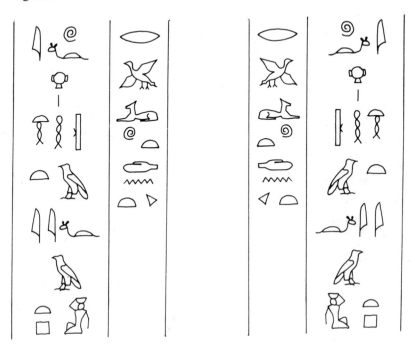

NUMERALS, FRACTIONS & TIME

The Egyptians developed a system of numbers at an early stage in their history. They were not the first to do so, but in the opinion of the author, the symbols they produced are possibly the most beautiful and artistic in the world. Here again, one should read them from left to right if the signs are looking to the left, and in this case, the higher values, that is, the thousands etc., would be on the left and the units on the right. Here follows a list of ancient Egyptian numerals up to one million. There are a few gaps because in some cases the hieroglyph is not known.

45

NUMERALS

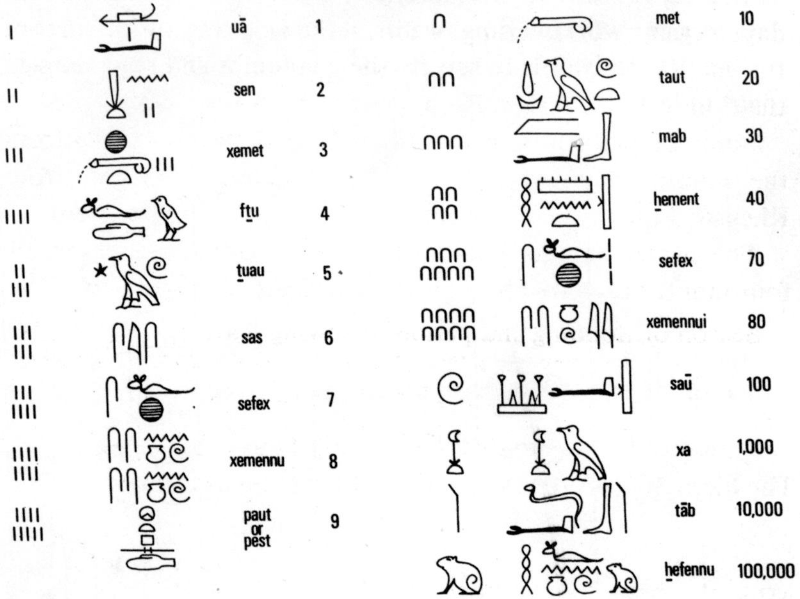

uā 1
sen 2
xemet 3
ftu 4
tuau 5
sas 6
sefex 7
xemennu 8
paut or pest 9
met 10
taut 20
mab 30
hement 40
sefex 70
xemennui 80
saū 100
xa 1,000
tāb 10,000
hefennu 100,000

Ordinal numbers are formed by either adding a sign, or putting one in front of the hieroglyphic group. In the case of 'four' we add a sign shaped like a little pot 'nu' which will produce 'fourth'. The same effect can be obtained by prefixing the number with giving the value of 'eighth'.

Fractions were expressed by using the symbol for 'mouth' = r underneath which was indicated the number called in English the denominator.

For instance, one would write one seventh like this.

Another example is

= 3 + 2/3 + 1/6 + 1/12 + 1/32

Large numbers are built up as follows

= 54,613

Time was measured in years, which consisted of 365 days; the year was subdivided into twelve months of thirty days each, and five intercalary days were added at the end. This was known as the 'civil' year. The period known as the Sothic year of 365¼ days began with the rising of Sirius, the Dog-star, on the first of the month of Thoth, when it coincided with the beginning of the flooding of the Nile. Each month was dedicated to a god.

Some of the Coptic names for the months were derived from the ancient language: Thoth is from Tehuti; Pachon from Khensu; Athor from Het-Heru, and Mesore is from Mes-Heru.

The twelve months were further divided into three seasons of four months each for the reasons of agriculture, thus:

Season of flooding and period of sowing = sat

Season of coming forth or growing = pert

Season of harvest and start of inundation = semut

The hieroglyphics for the division of time run as follows:

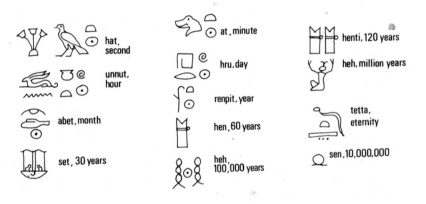

hat, second	
unnut, hour	at, minute
abet, month	hru, day
set, 30 years	renpit, year
	hen, 60 years
	heh, 100,000 years
henti, 120 years	
heh, million years	
tetta, eternity	
sen, 10,000,000	

So far, we have seen several examples of "the writing of the words of the god" — hieroglyphics. It will be recalled that two other kinds of script were used by the Egyptians, hieratic, the cursive writing of the priests and scribes, and the demotic or popular writing.

Here is an example of hieratic with its hieroglyphic counterpart.

A passage written in hieroglyphics (top) and, below, the same passage in hieratic.

Only constant practice would enable the student scribe to recognise the 'shorthand' version, but with the demotic script, one might think that this is even harder to read. At some early date (and again, we do not know when), the hieratic was streamlined and modified into the demotic, and it was used not only for business and social purposes, but also for publishing government decrees.

The Rosetta Stone, it will be remembered, had one of its sections inscribed in demotic. Here, though not from the Stone, is a line of demotic and the hieroglyphic transcript:

In order to satisfy the need for word-signs for every conceivable occasion and purpose, the government scribes invented thousands of beautifully-drawn figures and shapes. These include men and women, gods and goddesses, members of the body, animals, birds, fish, reptiles, insects, plants, parts of buildings, ships, furniture, apparel, arms and armour and many others.

In the limits of this book it is impossible to set before the reader a full list, indeed, it is not necessary and would be merely tiring for him. However, the following sets of figures will give some idea of the tremendous vocabulary needed by the scribe in temple or government service, or as teacher.

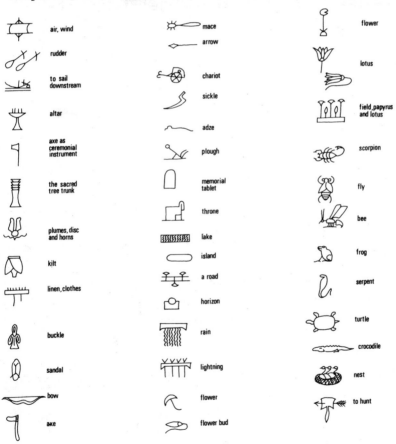

air, wind	mace	flower
rudder	arrow	lotus
to sail downstream	chariot	
altar	sickle	field, papyrus and lotus
axe as ceremonial instrument	adze	scorpion
the sacred tree trunk	plough	fly
plumes, disc and horns	memorial tablet	bee
kilt	throne	frog
linen, clothes	lake	serpent
buckle	island	turtle
sandal	a road	crocodile
bow	horizon	nest
axe	rain	to hunt
	lightning	
	flower	
	flower bud	

49

Having digested this brief but somewhat formidable list, and perhaps having learned something of the Egyptian alphabet, the reader is invited to compare this short extract from an inscription of King Pepi I with the hieroglyphs he has learned and to detect the sounds represented by the various signs.

Short extract from an inscription of King Pepi I (VI Dynasty)

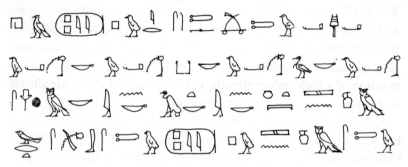

TRANSLATION

Hail Pepi this! Rise up thou, stand up. Pure art thou, pure is thy double, pure is thy soul, pure is thy power. Cometh to thee thy mother, cometh to thee Nut, the fashioner great, she purifieth thee, O Pepi this, she fashioneth thee.

Much of the literature of ancient Egypt available to us is of a religious character and perhaps the most important is the collection of chapters known as The Book of the Dead; its correct name is "per em hru" – "Coming forth by Day" and, as already indicated, a copy of this work, or at least extracts from it, was an essential item that had to accompany the dead person if he was to reach the Elysian Fields and enjoy eternal life.

As far back as the XIIth dynasty (BC 2500), extracts from it were written in the hieratic script upon sarcophagi and this practice was maintained right up to the second century AD. Selections in hieroglyphic script together with painted scenes covered the walls of the tombs of royalty, government officials, priests and other people of rank and position.

Large scrolls containing beautifully illustrated chapters were buried with them. Some parts of the book "Coming forth by Day" are so incredibly ancient that as long ago as BC 3500, the scribes were themselves unable to understand it all, but continued to copy what they saw and pass it on.

Not all the papyri in national collections are of a religious character; some contain stories, like that of the "Eloquent Peasant", there are work-songs, love songs, and songs to be sung at banquets; several papyri deal with medical matters and mathematical problems, and there is the so-called 'wisdom literature'. It is pleasant to record that many of the latter contain moral maxims of a high order; already in those ancient days, kindliness and desire for justice had long been stirring in men's hearts.

Several of the writings show clearly the duty a man owes to his god and to his fellow beings. One says regarding sacrifices: "More acceptable is the character of a just man than the ox of the evil-doer"; another "Do not at any time be evil or cruel, for kindness is good. Make your monument to be lasting through your neighbour's love of you."

A fifth dynasty king tells his aging vizier how to instruct his son so that he can better serve the throne, for "there is no one born wise". The son must learn to "be not proud because you are better educated, be not over-confident because you are better informed. Take counsel with the ignorant man as with the learned".

The artistic beauty of the hieroglyphics

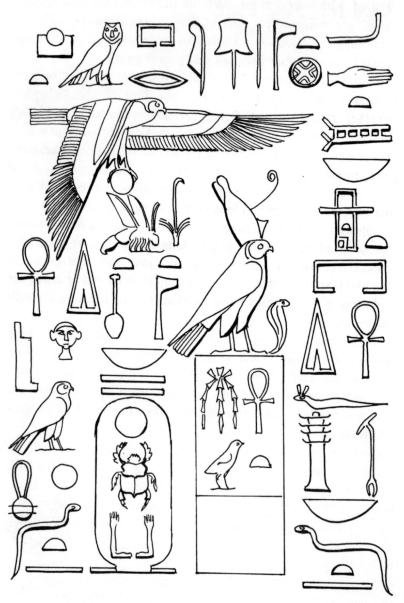

Name and titles of Sesostris I — XII Dynasty

Chapter 5

NOTES ON THE RELIGION AND GODS OF ANCIENT EGYPT

The religious beliefs of the Egyptians were basically the same throughout their history, but as time passed there came into being a bewildering pantheon of gods and goddesses. The reason for this was that often the attributes of one god were applied to another, or perhaps the cult of one special favourite declined in favour of another; sometimes, too, new gods arose and became popular in a district and their influence spread.

The oldest god of Egypt is Heru, and his symbol is the hawk or falcon. The great Sun-god Ra or Amen-Ra was supposed to be the creator of all things; he appeared in many other forms such as an ithyphallic mummy, a ram-headed, goose-headed or scarab-beetle-headed man. He was self-created, and possessed every kind of attribute, natural and spiritual. It is possible that the Egyptians had formulated at quite an early date the idea and belief in the One God. The ancient Egyptians, the Greeks, and Christians everywhere would, at least, have one thing in common no matter how much they disagreed about the basic corner-stones of their respective faiths — that the origin of the world was born out of Chaos. The first few lines of the Chapter of Genesis tells us: "In the beginning, God created the heaven and the earth. And the earth was without form, and void; and darkness was on the face of the deep . . . . . . And God said, Let there be light: and there was light . . . ."

The Greeks believed that the world began in the form of a shapeless mass ruled by a deity called Chaos, whose appearance could not be described, as there was no light by which he could be seen.

His wife, the dark goddess of night, called Nyx, wore black robes, and her countenance was said to be as black as her dress. Aeons passed, and the pair began to weary of their dark existence, so they called in their son Erebus (Darkness) to aid them.

The first thing he did was to cast his father from the throne, and the next was to marry his mother. Two beautiful children were born to them, Aether (Light) and Hemera (Day). These two in turn dethroned their parents and ruled supreme. Then followed, through the aid of their child Eros (Love) the creation of the earth, the heavens, and the sea.

Since the earliest times, the Egyptians possessed three distinct cosmogonies based on the traditions of three cities: Heliopolis, Hermopolis, and Memphis. According to the beliefs of the first-named, our world began as a watery chaotic mass called Nun. From this, the god Atum emerged and appeared on a mound. Inexplicably, he came into existence by himself. We are told that Atum, in his Beauty, thrust his phallus into his hand, excited desire and brought forth his seed which he placed into his mouth and swallowed. From this primeval act, the god Shu (who represented the air we breathe) and the goddess Tefnut (who represented the water which surrounded the earth) were born.

According to the logical Egyptians, Atum was self-generating, but Shu and Tefnut together brought forth Geb (Earth) and Nut, (the Sky), who in their turn bore Osiris, Isis, Set and Nephthys.

These Personages formed the Divine Ennead, the Company of Nine. According to the Hermopolitan idea of Creation, which also had the Chaotic tradition, a mound arose from the watery mass upon which a giant egg appeared; from this egg emerged the Sun-god.

In Memphis, which became the capital city of Egypt, the third form of tradition arose. Ptah, the city's principal god, was made to become, possibly for political reasons, the original creator-god, and the all-powerful priests formulated a new legend

54

about the beginning of things.

Although Ptah was now the Great Creator, eight other gods were contained within him, and according to the Memphites Ptah first conceived the world then "created it with his own word".

Is this not markedly similar to the account of the Creation in the Bible? "Let there be light . . . ."

Nevertheless, for all attempts to provide a clear explanation, Egyptian theology is a very confusing business, partially due to the existence of the three cosmogonies, the gaining or waning in popularity of certain gods in various cities over scores of centuries, and to the fact that the attributes of one god were contained in another, for example, both the hawk-headed and scarab-headed gods are identified with Ra, as Amen-Ra is with the ithyphallic gods Min, Amsu and Atum.

The symbol of Amen-Ra was the sun, and the Egyptians believed him to be the father of Osiris, and that Osiris was his only son. Osiris, being of divine origin and perfect, reigned on earth both wisely and well, until he was murdered by Set, who among the gods represented the powers of evil and darkness.

He rose from the dead, became the god of the Underworld, and because he suffered, died and rose from the dead, he became the absolute symbol of the Resurrection to the ancient Egyptians who planted all their hopes for everlasting life upon this shattering event. And so, since earliest times, when real tombs of brick or stone began to be built, the preserved dead were placed in them with everything they would need until the day of resurrection should dawn.

To the Egyptians, a person was composed of nine different parts:

a body, *khat*

a soul, *ba*

a double, *ka*

a form, *sekhem*

a heart, *ab*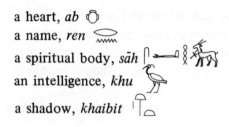
a name, *ren*
a spiritual body, *sāh*
an intelligence, *khu*
a shadow, *khaibit*

After death the body, separated from those parts that would corrupt quickly such as the intestines, liver and the brain, was embalmed according to custom, wrapped in hundreds of yards of linen in which were inserted various charms and amulets, and placed in its tomb, where it awaited visits from its soul in the form of a man-headed bird, the ba.

Isis or Aset was the mother of Horus and the wife of Osiris, while Asar was the daughter of the Sky-goddess Nut. Her sister Nephthys and her brother Set married, and in due course this couple, out of jealousy, plotted against the life of Osiris. The story of the murder and mutilation of Osiris by Set is an ancient and colourful one, and we are indebted to Sir E W Budge's extraction from Plutarch's work on the subject.

"Osiris reigned over the land of Egypt, and at once applied himself to the task of teaching his people the arts of agriculture and the cultivation of the fruits of the earth; he gave them a wise body of laws and instructed them in the worship that must be paid to the gods. He also travelled widely about the world, inducing other peoples to yield to the strength of his reasoning, conveying it to them in the most agreeable manner by hymns and songs accompanied by musical instruments.

"While he was absent, Set tried to change the state of things according to his own desire, but Isis, who remained behind, was too vigilant and frustrated any evil attempt on the part of Set.

"One day, however, Osiris returned, and was invited to a great party to celebrate the occasion. In the hall stood a most beautiful chest of wood, painted and gilded in the most ornate manner.

"Everybody admired it, and Set, as if for a joke, promised to give the chest to anyone present whose body would fit it exactly. Now previously, Set had secretly taken the exact measurements of Osiris's body, and he knew only too well the course the matter would take.

"But to add to the fun and games, and to make it appear a genuine 'competition', the whole company, who were in the evil plot, laughingly tried their luck. Last of all, Osiris laid himself down in the chest, upon which the plotters clapped the cover on it, drove in the nails, and poured boiling lead over it.

"The conspirators then took the chest to the river and conveyed it to the sea, where they threw it in. As soon as Isis heard the terrible news, she cut off a lock of hair, put on mourning apparel and wandered about the land in search of the chest. As it happened, some children had seen what Set had done with the chest and where the plotters had disposed of it.

"Isis finally tracked it down to the coast at Byblos, where it had lodged in the branches of a tamarisk bush. Magically, this bush had swiftly grown into a large and beautiful tree, growing around the box and enclosing it on every side. The King of that place, amazed at the unusual sight, had cut down the tree and taken the part wherein the box was hidden to make a pillar to support the roof of his house.

"These things were made known to the goddess, and she went to Byblos, where the queen sent for her. So pleasant did she appear to the queen, that this lady made Isis a nurse to one of her sons.

"Some time later, Isis requested that the roof pillar might be given to her; this was done, and Isis, easily cutting it open, took out what she wanted. Then she threw herself upon the chest, making at the same time such loud and terrible lamentations that the younger of the king's sons died of fear. Taking the other boy with her, she set sail with the chest for Egypt. When she imagined herself to be alone in a deserted place, she opened the chest, embraced the corpse, and wept bitterly. But her

57

troubles were far from over; she hid the chest in a remote spot, but Set, one night out hunting by the light of the moon, accidently came upon it. Furious, he tore the body into pieces, fourteen in all, and scattered them up and down in different parts of the country.

"Poor Isis, when she discovered what had happened, set out once again in search of the scattered fragments of Osiris's body in a boat made of papyrus reeds. The light boat would travel more easily about the marshy parts of the country. [The reason why the Egyptians felt safe from crocodiles when in a papyrus boat was because one had once carried the goddess Isis.]

"Now some say that there are so many sepulchres to be found in Egypt relating to Osiris because whenever Isis found one of the scattered limbs, she buried it and set up a tomb. This story is contradicted by others who maintain that Isis merely presented each of the cities with a beautiful statue of Osiris in order that the honours due to his memory might be more widely spread over the land, and to frustrate the ruthless and evil searches of Set, who, if he finally succeeded in discovering the parts, might destroy them for ever.

"Now a war was about to take place between Set and Osiris's son Horus, and just about this time, Osiris returned from the Underworld and made himself known to his son. Great was the rejoicing at their meeting, the father cheerfully encouraging the young man for the battle to come, and at the same time teaching him the arts of war.

"Osiris asked Horus, 'What do you consider would be the finest thing you would have ever done in your life?' Horus answered at once, 'to avenge the wrongs committed against my father and mother'.

"Osiris rejoiced and his heart became glad at these words. And now the battle lines were drawn up and the terrible encounter, which was to last for many days, began. Bitterly the two sides fought, and for some time neither could claim the victory. Finally, however, the troops of Horus gradually overcame the

58

enemy and Set was taken prisoner and committed to the custody of Isis. For some reason, Isis, instead of ordering Set's execution for the terrible crime he had committed, set him free. When Horus heard about this, he became mad with fury, rushed up to his mother and tore off from her head the royal crown and insignia. This rash act offended the gods, and Thoth at once stepped forward and replaced the crown with a helmet shaped like the head of an ox."

According to the story, two more battles were fought between the opposing forces, and in both Set had the worst of it. This story is surely the prototype showing the fight between good and evil which is preached in our churches even today. The Christian church offers proof of the Saviour's triumph over Satan, but Christianity is not the only religion which supports the good and condemns evil things; almost all faiths take the same stand.

The Egyptians firmly believed that some days were lucky and that others were definitely unlucky; in their calendar one special day of the year, the 26th day of the month of Thoth, was regarded as "thrice times unlucky", for that was the day when Horus battled with Set. Egyptians were advised to avoid enterprises of all kinds, and to do absolutely nothing on that day.

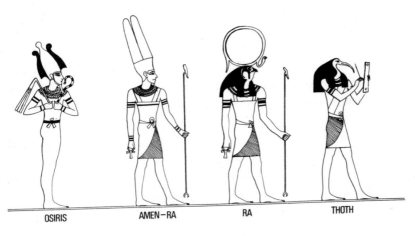

OSIRIS   AMEN–RA   RA   THOTH

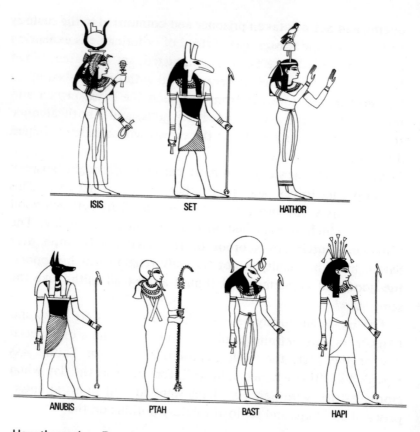

ISIS SET HATHOR

ANUBIS PTAH BAST HAPI

How the ancient Egyptians saw their gods; the drawings depict some of the most powerful, beloved and adored gods and goddesses in the land of Egypt.

As will be seen from the illustrations, the Egyptians portrayed their gods and goddesses in a most attractive form according to their own canon or laws of art; the manner in which they drew the human form may seem somewhat strange to someone unfamiliar with the Egyptian art form. The head was always drawn in profile, and was attached to a frontal aspect of the shoulders, arms and chest, which narrowed down to a three-quarter view of the hips. From here and downwards to the feet, the body again assumed a profile or side view.

60

Although the face was shown in profile, the eye was drawn as from the front, giving the face in most cases a most appealing expression. It might be asked, could not the Egyptians draw the human figure in the normal way? Well, they certainly could, in fact they had to when they prepared sketches from which to make a sculptured figure of one of their kings. When Akhnaten, the heretic king, moved his court to Akhetaten (the modern Tell-el-Amarna), the artists of the day moved away somewhat from the time-honoured laws of drawing and became more 'liberal', founding a new 'school' of art.

Returning to our list of gods, I have always found Thoth (or Tehuti), the ibis-headed god, one of the most interesting; he is 'The Measurer', the Scribe of the Gods, the measurer of time, the inventor of numbers and the Art of Writing. In the Judgement Hall of Osiris, it is he who stands at the side of the great scales ready with his palette and reed to record the result of the weighing of the heart announced by jackal-headed Anubis (Anpu) who scrupulously checks the balance.

Anubis is the god of the dead and is always shown wearing the black jackal mask; in the ceremonies attached to the process of mummification, one of the officiating priests wore this headgear of a black jackal, black being the colour of rebirth.

Ptah is one of the oldest of the gods and his worship at Memphis dates from the time of the first dynasty. He is always represented in the form of a mummy holding a triple sceptre composed of symbols for Life, Strength, and Stability.

Bast, the cat-headed goddess, had a magnificent temple erected in her honour at Bubastis. The cat was greatly revered in ancient Egypt, to such an extent in fact that anyone killing a cat by accident suffered severe penalties; if the killing was deliberate, the villain paid for it with his life.

Her sister goddess, Sekhet, has the head of a lioness and represents the scorching heat of the sun.

Khepera, known as the Creator, is the scarab-headed god; he is associated with Ptah, and is said to have created himself.

According to the legends, he is the father of Shu and Tefnut. The former is the god of air, and is always shown paired with the latter, the goddess of moisture.

Min, or Amsu, was the god of fertility and is depicted as an ithyphallic human figure holding aloft a flail. This god was identified by the Greeks with Pan, and was worshipped at Khemmis, the ancient Egyptian town famous in those days for its weavers of fine linen and its stone cutters.

Maāt, the goddess of Truth and Law, is shown as a woman wearing a vertical feather upon her head.

Khonsu is the god of the Moon, sometimes represented as a man, or sometimes shown as a hawk-headed man wearing the lunar disc and crescent. He is associated with Amen-Ra and the goddess Mut in the Theban Triad and was worshipped with great honour at Thebes.

Imhotep, it will be remembered, was the chief minister of King Zoser and the architect of the Step Pyramid at Saqqara. He became venerated as the god of Medicine and Learning in Egypt, was accepted by the Greeks in the same capacity and given the name of Askleipios.

Mut, one of the divinities of the Theban Triad, was the divine wife of Amen; she is shown as a woman, and her sign is the vulture.

Hathor, or Athor, is called the Lady of the Sycamore, and the Lady of the West, and often appears in the form of a cow emerging from the Theban Hills. She is usually shown as a woman wearing the head-dress of the cow with the sun's disc between the horns. The Greeks knew her as Aphrodite.

Sebek was the crocodile god worshipped at Kom Ombos and in the Fayum.

Ammit is the fearsome creature composed of part hippopotamus, part lion and part crocodile who stands waiting at the scales to devour the hearts of those who have been found wanting in Truth.

Bes is possibly the only human figure drawn from the front.

He is the dwarf-god, the protector against snakes, and is associated with childbirth.

Hapi is the great god of the Nile, sometimes shown with woman's breasts, and coloured red and green to represent the colours of the waters of the Nile just before and just after the start of the inundation. He wears a crown of papyrus flowers.

Set, the wicked one, was the brother of the great god Osiris and his slayer. The Greeks called him Typhon, and he is shown wearing the head-dress of an animal resembling an okapi.

The Egyptians believed that after a man had died he was taken to the Great Hall of Osiris, the Judge of the Dead, and that his conscience, in the form of his heart, was weighed in the heavenly scales. The illustration shows the deceased dressed in pure raiment, his heart upon one pan of the scales, while the feather of Truth stands in the other. Squatting on top of the beam is the dog-headed ape, the companion of Thoth, the Scribe of the Gods. Jackal-headed Anubis kneels to scrutinise the indicator of the balance, and Thoth himself stands ready to record the result of the weighing.

Hungrily, Ammit waits to devour the faulty heart, but usually she is cheated out of her meal, thanks to the uprightness of that organ. Usually this cermony is performed in the company of a number of gods and goddesses as witnesses, such as Horus, Hathor, Seb, Heru-khuti, Shu and Tefnut.

The deceased does not stand silent while his fate is being determined by the Weighers; in his own defence he begs that there shall be no resistance to him in his judgement or opposition to him from the Divine Chiefs and that no lies shall be spoken against him in the presence of the god.

According to the Book of the Dead, the dead man in the Hall of Judgement always assumed the name of Osiris, and now all the company has seen that the heart and feather have balanced to a nicety. Thoth steps forward and says, "Hear ye all this judgement. The heart of Osiris has in very truth been weighed

The weighing of the heart of the scribe Ani by Anubis while Thoth records the result. The monster Ammit stands ready to devour the heart should it fail to pass the test. Above, sitting in judgement, is the Company of the Gods.

A section from the Papyrus of Anhai presenting another artist's view of the weighing of the heart. Notice that while Anubis checks the balance with scrupulous care he appears to be holding one of the strings!

and his soul has stood witness for him; his trial in the Great Balance is true. There has not been found any wickedness in him; he has not wasted the offerings in the temples; he has not harmed anyone by his acts; he has not uttered slanderous reports while he was upon earth."

Now the heavenly company confirm the words of Thoth, "What you have proclaimed cannot be denied. Osiris is just and righteous; he has not committed any sin, neither has he done evil against us. Ammit shall not be allowed to prevail over him; he shall be allowed to enter into the presence of the Great God Osiris, and offerings of meat and drink shall be made to him, together with an abiding home in Sekhet-hetepu as is given to the followers of Horus."

After these gladsome tidings, the hawk-headed god Horus leads the deceased into the presence of Osiris himself, who sits in splendour within a shrine. He wears the *atef* crown and in his hands he grasps the insignia of sovereignty, the crook, the sceptre and the flail of Royal Egypt. Supporting him from behind are the goddesses Isis and Nephthys, while standing on a lotus flower at the feet of the god are the four deities known as the children of Horus. In this context they represent the four cardinal points. Several papyri exist containing illustrations of the scenes we are describing but with certain variations; this one, perhaps the best of its kind, is the papyrus of the scribe Ani, and a very beautiful piece of colourful work it is. The colours blend so well with the tawny papyrus, and the whole thing is a joy to behold.

The deceased scribe Ani now kneels before the throne of Osiris upon a reed mat; he now wears a whitened wig on top of which sits a cone of fragrant ointment. With his right hand he adores the god; in his left, he holds the *kherp* sceptre. In front of Ani is a table piled up with offerings of food, drink and flowers which presumably he will share with the god.

Hawk-headed Horus says to Osiris, "I have come to you, O Unnefer, and I have brought the Osiris Ani to you. His heart is righteous in the balance and it has not committed any sin against the gods. Thoth has weighed it, and it is very true and righteous. Grant to Ani offerings of meat and drink, allow him to enter into the presence of Osiris and grant that he may be like unto the followers of Horus for ever."

Kneeling glorified before the Great God, Ani says, "O Lord of the Underworld, I am in your presence . . . There is no sin in my body, I have uttered no lies, I have done nothing with a double motive. Grant that I may be like the favoured beings who stand about you, and that I may be an Osiris greatly favoured of the beautiful god and beloved of the Lord of the World, I who am in truth a royal scribe loving him, Ani, victorious in judgement before the god Osiris!"

We next see Ani employing his days in the Sekhet-hetepu, the Elysian Fields, adoring various gods, making offerings, paddling his papyrus boat which contains a table loaded with offerings; he ploughs the rich black earth; he sows, reaps and winnows the splendid harvest of wheat that grows alongside a stretch of pure water.

Nobody looked forward to carrying out these agricultural tasks after death, and to avoid them, little stone, wooden or procelain figures, called *ushabti*, were placed in the tomb to do the work for them. By pronouncing certain words of power, these figures would come to life ready to take over the field labours so distasteful to the deceased.

Having got rid of the hard unpleasant tasks, the deceased could now look forward to a time of tolerable bliss, but his troubles were not yet over. After death, the soul had a large number of enemies to overcome, and if he happened to be unfamiliar with their names, or forgot the words of power, he was in danger of annihilation. For example, in the Hall of Osiris there dwelt the forty-two gods, and to each one the dead man's soul had to swear that he had not committed any of the Forty-two sins. Here are some examples from the 'Negative Confession'.

"O Akhi, who comest forth from Nu, I have never been arrogant in speech."

"O Eyes of Flame, who come forth from Seaut, I have never stolen the property of the gods."

"O thou god whose face is turned behind thee, who comest forth from my shrine, I have never caused anyone to weep tears of sadness."·

"O thou what observest what hath been brought into the temple of Amsu, I have never defiled myself."

"O Reciter of words who comest forth from Urit, I have never spoken in hot anger."

In several of the others, the deceased denies that he has committed murder, theft, acts of violence, caused terror, lied, conspired against others or committed any acts of uncleanliness.

Apparently, his affirmations are accepted, and he is passed as being without sin. In the Hall of Osiris are many mansions, and the deceased cannot enter until he has answered questions put to him by the doors, the fastenings, the bolts, the doorposts; even the very floor will not allow him to walk upon it until he has announced its secret name, but needless to say, the dead man's soul passes all the tests with honours.

The beliefs of the ancient Egyptians were compounded of both religion and magic, and their devotion to their innumerable religious ceremonies earned for them among foreigners the reputation of being both the most pious and the most superstitious of nations.

Chapter 6

FUNERARY CUSTOMS

A great deal of our knowledge about Egypt and its literature springs directly from ancient customs associated with death, burial, and the preservation of the body. The layman, when he considers ancient Egypt, at once thinks of mummies and, in a way, he is quite right. Over an enormous period of time the bodies of most Egyptians underwent some process of preservation so that their souls could return to their bodies after the series of frightful combats in the Underworld.

'Mummy' is not an Egyptian word, either ancient or modern: it comes from the Arabic word *mumiya,* meaning bitumen or pitch. *Mumiyyet* is Arabic for a body preserved by bitumen, and although this substance was sometimes used in preserving human, animal and avian bodies in Egypt, many other substances such as resin, certain oils, aromatic gums and natron were used.

As noted in earlier chapters, Pre-dynastic burials consisted merely of burying the body in a shallow pit, the hot dry sand acting as a desiccating agent. Which came first, the discovery that bodies buried this way retained their human shape (although reduced to skin and bone), followed by a dawning belief in after-life and the development of funerary practices, *or* the development of the Resurrection idea followed by deliberate experiments to preserve the body as an abiding place for the soul?

The art of mummification really began towards the end of the Pre-dynastic Period and continued into Roman times. In the former, it was thought that the method of simple pit burial could be improved upon by enclosing the body in a wooden box, but the result produced the opposite effect — putrefaction instead of desiccation. The next step was to try wrapping the limbs in linen bandages in order to prevent the air affecting the corpse, but this, too, failed.

Many centuries were to pass before the secret was discovered; in order to prevent a body from decomposing, it was vital to remove the internal organs, at the same time dehydrating the body, head and limbs. Not until the period approaching the New Kingdom, 1567 BC, however, were these basic principles really understood by the embalmers.

Burials of the second dynasty provide evidence of a further step in the right direction. The embalmers realised the difficulties attached to the task of preventing the forces of corruption attacking the cadaver, and this step consisted of preserving the actual shape and features of the dead body by soaking the linen wrappings in some hot, resinous fluid and moulding them upon head and features, around the limbs, the fingers and toes, upon the breasts and nipples, and the genital organs. Fingernails, toenails and every other detail of the body was brought out in perfect form. The result was a hard shell of lacquered linen, and those which have been found have kept their shape to a wonderful degree.

In most cases, the body was laid to rest in the contracted position, but I have seen at least one example where the body lies at full length. Inside its shell, the body would decompose and shrink, leaving little more than the skeleton, but the original shape and features of the person would remain, as indeed many have done.

A great deal of our knowledge of the way in which the dead were mummified comes from the Greek historians. Herodotus, who visited Egypt, tells us that the art was carried on by a guild or corporate body of men licensed by law.

Basically, there were three grades of mummification which were governed by price and the rank of the dead person. With bodies of the first grade, the brain was extracted through the nose by means of an iron instrument which punctured the ethnoid bone. After this, the internal organs were taken from the body through an incision made in the side with a sharp Ethiopian stone, the heart alone being left in position although, sometimes, it was removed, mummified and returned to the thoracic cavity. The next step was to dehydrate the body and the internal organs, which was achieved by steeping them in vessels containing natron, a compound of sodium bicarbonate and sodium carbonate in its dry state. This substance occurs naturally in Egypt, and the body spent some seventy days immersed in its dry-salt bath.

When all was ready, the viscera were placed in four special jars, sometimes called 'Canopic jars'. These organs were under the protection of the four sons of Horus; into the Qebhsenuef (hawk-headed jar) went the intestines; the lungs into Hapi, (ape-headed); the stomach into Duamutef (jackal-headed) and into Imseti or Mestha (man-headed), the liver. The spaces in the body left by the removal of the organs were packed with linen and any other materials to hand, and the incision sutured together. (At some time during the XXIst dynasty, it became the practice to replace the viscera in the body instead of in the jars).

Before wrapping, the body was treated with rare and secret oils which, in conjunction with special prayers and words of power uttered by the officiating priests, were supposed to impart such a sweet odour that the deceased's face would neither change nor perish, and which "would make its members perfect".

Amulets made of gold, silver, lapis-lazuli, turquoise and crystal were enclosed among the first bandages; each one had the certain property of protecting various parts of the body. Nothing was to be left to chance in case the dead person was placed at risk; in fact, the anointing ceremony was repeated.

Many short bandages were also at hand to be laid and fastened about the head by a priest wearing the black jackal head-dress representing Anubis, the god of the dead; there were twenty-two pieces of bandage to the right and to the left of the face

71

passing over the two ears, and many of these pieces bore a drawing of a god or part of a god.

Then began the general bandaging of the body, beginning with the fingers of the left hand and arms, followed by similar treatment of the right. Then came the toes, feet and legs, working upwards to the base of the trunk; the penis was wrapped separately, and placed in the erect position. It is probable that these ceremonies, if carried out in a correct manner, would require several days, and it was only the really wealthy families who could afford the great expense of the priests' services, the hundreds of yards of fine linen bandages, the rare oils and ingredients, etc., not to mention the elaborate services at the tomb and the cost of the tomb itself.

The most important ceremony of all, called the 'Opening of of the Mouth and Eyes' was usually performed in a chamber near the entrance to the tomb, or at a spot which had been specially consecrated.

Quite a large number of people took part; several priests, the immediate relatives of the deceased, two women who represented Isis and Nephthys, and a group symbolising the armed guard of Horus. The ceremony was of great antiquity and represented happenings which took place at the funeral of Osiris.

A representation of the scene at the tomb can be seen in the papyrus of Hunnefer in the British Museum. At the right is a pyramidal building representing the tomb, next to which is a round-topped stela with prayers to Osiris; Anubis is shown supporting the mummy, while two female figures mourn for the dead.

The priest standing on the far left by a table of offerings is burning some sweet-smelling incense in a censer held in his left hand; a flask of sacred fluid, perhaps holy water, is in his right.

Two young priests are shown performing the actual ceremony of Opening the Mouth with iron instruments shaped like the adze, and a snake-shaped object having the head of a ram. The

Papyrus of Hunnefer, XIXth Dynasty, 1300 BC. Opening the mouth.

drawing below shows the poor animals slaughtered for the sacrifice, indeed the calf has already lost a leg and its heart, which will be offered to the mouth of the mummy. Below, right, stands the table with the various objects for use in the ceremony; the adze-like articles called Seb-ur and Tuntet; the sacrificial meat; the instrument called Pesh-en-kef which has the power of opening the jaw-bones so that the dead man can recover the gift of speech; several jars and other vessels and the leopard-skin worn by the chief priest.

The cost of the mummifying process alone would have amounted to about £1000.

Herodotus tells us that in the second method of preservation, the brain was left intact, and that the intestines were dissolved and removed in a fluid state. As in the first method, the body would lie for seventy days in the dry-salt bath which would reduce it to nothing but skin and bones. This method was much

73

cheaper, but there were the added costs of the services of the priests and, of course, the tomb.

The third method was for the use of the poor and was a very simple one. A strong astringent was injected into the body which had the power of contracting the internal organs; the corpse itself was steeped in the natron for the seventy-day period, and, we assume, was collected by the relatives for swathing in any kind of linen wrappings they could obtain. This method, Herodotus says, cost very little.

Bodies were taken to the embalmers to be mummified as soon as possible after death; the exception to this was in the case of beautiful young women who had died. Their journey to the embalmers' premises was sometimes delayed for a few days to prevent the possibility of indignities being offered to the corpse by a depraved employee of the establishment.

We have very little information about such establishments, how they were laid out, what security precautions were in force, or even in what kind of buildings the work was carried on. We must assume that they were permanent erections of stone, having doors and windows for ventilation, for the odours emanating from such premises must have been perfectly horrible. Notwithstanding the deeply religious associations, the work of the mummifiers was extremely unpleasant. One can picture the long rows and tiers of receptacles, each docketed and containing the well-salted remains of the populace's loved ones; the chief clerk's office with its pigeon-holes filled with papyri, all neatly rolled up and containing details of client, relatives' addresses, chosen method of embalmment, how much paid on account and in what form; the reception hall, suitably decorated with wall-paintings to impress the customer and to produce suitable feelings of awe and piety; the linen store-rooms; the carpenters' workshop and the mummifiers themselves engaged upon their grisly tasks.

To the Egyptian, however, the work was neither horrible nor grisly; people were born, they lived, they died, and when this happened, their bodies had to be made ready for the beautiful life to come. The public at large were only too grateful to the priests and embalmers for the irreplaceable services they rendered to the dead.

Chapter 7

THE POWER OF ART IN MAGIC AND RELIGION

From previous chapters it is clear that the men of Egypt believed it possible to bring to life, by means of certain formulae, words of power, drawings and paintings, any figure of a god, man or animal, or even a well-loaded table of offerings. In the tombs of the wealthy during the early dynasties, complete meals, or the remains of them, have been found, but as time passed, people ceased to load the tombs of their relatives with real food, drink, weapons and games, and began to put their trust into written texts and words of power as well as paintings which would, at the required times, turn into realities.

This is not to say that after a certain date, nobody placed real food or other articles in the tombs; it was done quite frequently, right through Egyptian history, but generally the majority of folk were content to trust in the efficiency of the written word and in the accompanying drawings and paintings.

The dead man's *ka* or double needed nourishment, and if it did not find it in the shape of a model altar with model bread, meat, cakes, flasks of water and beer, or even a poor little altar with drawings of these viands upon it, the *ka* would be forced to wander about looking for sustenance and picking up filth to eat and foul water to drink. In the 52nd Chapter of the Book of the Dead, the deceased prays that he shall not have to eat filth, which is an abomination to him, instead of the cakes which are usually offered to Doubles. He dreads touching filth or having to take it into his hands. In the 189th Chapter, his prayer is that he shall not be obliged to drink foul water or to be defiled by it.

Before the custom came into being of placing texts written

on papyrus in the tombs, extracts from the Book of the Dead with illustrations were painted upon and inside the wooden coffins.

Being deprived of food and drink were not the only terrors of the deceased; what if he should lack air to breathe? A drawing overcame this dreadful risk, in which he is shown holding a little mast and sail, the symbol of wind, air, and breathing. He cries, "Hail, thou god Tem, grant thou unto me the sweet breath which dwelleth in my nostrils."

Among the pleasures anticipated by the deceased in the Underworld was the opportunity to sail across the vault of Heaven in the Boat of Ra accompanied by the great gods. How could this be achieved? A new piece of papyrus had to be obtained, and upon it a picture was drawn with special ink mixed with water of a boat in which were located the likenesses of Isis, Thoth, Khepera, Shu and the deceased. This picture had to be executed in a pure place, probably the temple and, when finished, the papyrus had to be fixed to the breast of the dead man in such a way that it had no actual contact with his body. Subsequently, by the recitation of certain words of power uttered over the picture in the correct tone of voice, this longed-for pleasure would become a reality to the deceased during his sojourn in the Elysian Fields.

Some of our readers may find the use of pictures and 'words of power' rather amusing to contemplate in these modern times, but the principle still lives on as strong as ever. For example, when a couple get married, there is the priest or Registrar intoning the words, 'I pronounce you man and wife.' There are words of power for you! Again, at the launching of a ship, some VIP smashes a bottle of cheap champagne against the bows and says, 'May God bless all who sail in her!' Similarly, when a new building is being inaugurated, the mayor is usually asked to officiate at the stone-laying; the small block of limestone is lowered into position at which His Worship taps it with a trowel and pronounces the words, 'I declare this stone to be well and truly laid.'

On equal terms with the new piece of papyrus with the boat drawn upon it which enabled the ancient Egyptian to ride in the Boat of the Gods, the successful student of today obtains a similar document bearing some kind of design and a few lines of text saying he has obtained his 'O' or 'A' levels, has passed his music examination, or has the right to call himself a qualified engineer.

Such a document is real and important enough to the young man or woman of today; to the Egyptian, the little drawing of himself holding the sail was absolutely vital.

Words of power were not only used by priests and priest-magicians for the benefit of the dead, they were also employed by doctors and healers. If certain words, or Names of Power, were pronounced in the correct manner and with the proper intonation, the Egyptian doctor could heal the sick and cast out the evil spirits which he felt sure were responsible for causing the disease. Here is a commandment to be uttered by the healer in the presence of the patient; it is from the Ebers Medical Papyrus; "Flow out, fetid nose, flow out, son of fetid nose. Flow out, thou who breakest bones, destroyest the skull, diggest in the bone marrow and makest the seven holes in the head ill; go out to the ground, thou fetid one!" Medical treatment accompanied these words of power, but greater faith was placed in the latter.

Occasionally, the healer merely had to mention the *name* of a god to cause the evil spirit to abandon the sick body: "You fly before the conjuror, before the servant of Horus as soon as he mentions the name of Horus, or the name of Seth, the Lord of Heaven . . . you did die, and Horus has conquered the disease."

Often, in times of epidemics, a man could protect himself by reciting this formula: "I am the healthy one in the way of the passer-by. Shall I be smitten while I am healthy? . . . I am the one who has come forth out of the disaster."

It was thought extremely efficacious, when a doctor was

mixing and measuring out his potions, to speak the following words over the measuring vessel: "This measuring vessel is a vessel with which Horus measured his eye. Since that eye was correctly measured, life, health and happiness were found." The eye of Horus had a special significance in Egypt: in one of the battles with Set, Horus's eye had been torn to pieces, but Thoth completely restored it. Thereafter, the complete eye had come to mean, "whole, unharmed, unity" and the hieroglyphic sign represented these qualities, together with a measure of volume consisting of a little more than four and a half litres.

Regarding the present use of amulets or charms, it is not generally known that in most Jewish households there is to be found, just inside the front door upon one of the uprights, an object called a mazzuzah. This is a little piece of tin tacked on the wood at an angle, and inside it can be found a tiny roll of paper upon which is printed a prayer in Hebrew script for the protection of the house and inhabitants.

The use of various amulets worn not only by the dead but by the living was universal in Egypt, especially amulets of the scarab, the *Utchat* or Eye of Horus, the *nefer,* representing a lute and the *ankh,* the sign for 'life'. The idea of 'life' and 'fertility' were attached to the scarab because of its peculiar powers, and even today, it is said, Egyptian women dry the insect, crush it to powder, mix it with water and drink it to be assured of bearing large families.

Wearing the amulet of the Eye of Horus brought the blessings of strength, vigour and good health; the lute amulet lent itself very well in the design of necklaces and beads, and signified happiness and good luck. The origin of the shape of the ankh is unknown, but it represents 'life' or 'eternity', and wherever a god or goddess is portrayed on stone, wood or papyrus they are seen to be carrying one. In Latin, it is known as the *crux anxata.*

Returning to the subject of art as a living power, the painted coffins of all the periods in Egyptian history are of great interest, from the massive wooden constructions of early times to the beautifully decorated body-shaped mummy cases of the XVIIIth to XXIInd dynasties. Regarding the latter, I have before me two coloured photographs; the first is the coffin of Hu-en-Amen, an incense bearer in the temple of Amen at Thebes, dating from about BC 1150, and it is exquisitely painted with figures of Osiris, Hathor, Isis, Nephthys, Anubis and Horus. The head-dress is painted in the form of wings, and there is a wide decorated collar extending down below the shoulders. The hands are crossed and apparently hold the sceptre and flail. Below this, in the region of the stomach, the deceased in the form of Osiris stands guarded by the outstretched wings of Isis and Nephthys and a pair of Utchat eyes.

Below this, at either side, the deceased adores the gods Horus and scarab-headed Khepera, while under this scene, Hathor, in the form of the sacred cow, emerges from the Western Hills.

Not an inch has been wasted; every figure, every line and every posture is loaded with meaning. It is not decoration for its own sake, not merely a beautiful coffin through which to do honour to the deceased; the whole thing acts as a powerful talisman to guarantee the safety and ever-living of this incense bearer, Hu-en-Amen.

The second photograph is of the mummy case of a priestess, Thent-mut-s-Kebti, probably of the XXIInd dynasty, and also from Thebes. Again, there is the wing-painting on the head-dress, but instead of a collar, there are two more pairs of wings, the larger, on the chest, growing from a large black scarab.

Below this is a scene in which the priestess (a very young-looking girl indeed) is led into the presence of Osiris in the form of a mummy by hawk-headed Horus. Before him springs a large lotus upon which stand the four children of Horus. To the left, bearing outsize ankhs, stand Isis, Nephthys and two other goddesses which are not too clear. In the section below this scene, two sets of beautiful wings guard two rams, while below this, there is a splendid tableau with the Tet (the tree-trunk in which Osiris's body was found by Isis) surmounted by the atef crown and holding the sceptre and flail being saluted by Isis and Nephthys. Under this picture, we see the little priestess kneeling surrounded by a stronghold of ankhs, while Horus and Thoth support two large flasks from which pour the stream of ankhs.

This last is a very powerful picture indeed, and its meaning is obvious; eternal, but eternal life will be enjoyed by the little priestess, for Horus-the-Avenger-of-his-Father and the Mighty Measurer have taken upon themselves the beautiful task of pouring a constant stream of eternity over the kneeling figure. What could befall her in the Underworld after this?

In the early part of this century when Egyptology was in its youth, it was generally thought that the Egyptians were a sombre people, obsessed with death, funerary customs and after-life. This state of thought probably came about because the majority of finds in archaeological excavations happened to be funerary objects from tombs; coffins; wall-paintings in tombs; prayers and religious texts for the benefit of the dead, etc. If all these things had not been well hidden, and if the tombs had been less indestructible, there would have been even less material available to the picks of our archaeologists.

We must therefore not run away with the idea that the Egyptians were a sad race of people, forever mourning the dead. Their main concern was to take all possible steps to ensure that in the next world, a world in which they fervently believed, they would be resurrected, reborn, and if all the right words were uttered in the right tones, would enjoy the beautiful life of laughter, happiness, plentiful food and drink, music and love in company with "the beautiful gods".

From wall-paintings and other sources we have plenty of evidence that the Egyptians enjoyed many kinds of games; wrestling was a popular pastime; fishing and hunting, together with fowling in the marshes, were the pleasures of the well-to-do, and parties, where much wine and beer were drunk and musicians played, were always a great favourite. To become helplessly drunk was frowned upon, but to be tipsily merry added to the fun. Everybody was expected to enjoy themselves to the full; sometimes it was the custom to parade a small coffin among the guests, to remind them to "make the most of today, for tomorrow we die".

Regarding words of power and magic, which were such important features in Egyptian life, it would be appropriate to end this chapter with a story that comes from a papyrus of the Ptolemaic period. It concerns a prince, Setnau Kha-em-Uast, himself a skilled magician who had great knowledge of secret magical formulae and religious literature, and who was fully conversant with the contents of the library of magical books; in short, he was a sorcerer. One day, the story goes, he was discussing various aspects of the power of the spoken and written word with some of the king's wise men, when to his annoyance, they laughed at him in disbelief.

To the man who laughed loudest, Setnau said, "If you would like to read a book which can conjure the spirits of the dead and many other wonderful things, come with me and you can yourself behold it. It was written by Thoth himself, and it contains two formulae. The recital of the first will enchant the heavens, the earth, hell, sea and mountains, and by it you will see all the birds, reptiles and fish, for its power will bring the fish to the top of the water. The recital of the second will enable a man if he be in the tomb to take the form which he had on earth." Still smiling in disbelief, Setnau's companion asked where this terrible book was to be found, and Setnau answered, "In the tomb of Ptah-nefer-ka at Memphis."

Shortly after, Setnau and his brother went to this place in order to search for the tomb, and after seeking it for three days, they found it on the third. The sorcerer recited some words over it, and a fissure appeared in the earth. The brothers stepped down and entered the tomb which was dazzlingly illuminated by the radiance that emanated from the Book.

To the brothers' amazement, not only Ptah-nefer-ka was present in the tomb, but also his wife Ahura, and their son Merhu.

82

Why was this? Both mother and son had died and had been buried at Coptos, but their 'doubles' had come to reside with Ptah-nefer-ka through the power of the ibis-headed god Thoth.

"Why have you come to disturb us?" asked Ptah-nefer-ka. Setnau answered that he had come in order to obtain the Book, but the wife Ahura set up a wailing and begged him to desist because of the calamities which had befallen her family already.

To the brothers she related the circumstances of the terrible misfortunes that had occurred since they had had possession of it. First, she said, she was the brother of Ptah-nefer-ka; they had fallen in love, had married, and she bore a son, Merhu. After this, her husband had given up all other occupations in order to study the magical books. Finding his researches somewhat disappointing and failing to produce the powerful effects for which he was striving, he met a priest who promised to reveal the actual spot where the mighty Book of Thoth might be found.

For this service the priest required payment of a large amount of silver and two finely decorated coffins. When these goods had been paid over, the wife continued, the priest directed her husband to search at a spot in the middle of the river at Coptos. There the Book, the Scroll of Wisdom, giving the reciter of its chapters power over the earth and the heavens, was to be found in an iron box. The iron box was in a bronze box, the bronze box was in a box of palm-tree wood, this wooden box was in a box made of ebony and ivory, the ebony and ivory box was in a silver box, and the silver was in a golden box. Continuing her tale, the wife went on, "this is the Book that has been responsible for the terrible misfortunes ending in the deaths of my husband, my son, and myself. The box was surrounded by serpents and scorpions, and coiled around the box was a huge snake which no weapon could harm".

According to the story (which, by the way, has no satisfactory conclusion), Ptah-nefer-ka told the king about these wonders, and the king provided him with a royal barge for the journey to

Coptos. Ptah-nefer-ka went with his wife and son to the temple of Isis upon their arrival and offered up sacrifices to the goddess in order to obtain her help and blessing in the enterprise. As the journey was under the aegis of the king, the high priest caused to be made a model of a raft and several figures of workmen holding various tools.

The priest himself was no mean magician, for we are told that he recited certain "words of power" over the little raft and the figures, upon which the raft became a real full-sized object and the figures became living men. Now the search for the nest of boxes began in earnest, but it was not until three days and nights had passed that it was discovered. It was fished up to the surface, and found to be, as prophesied, covered with serpents and scorpions which Ptah-nefer-ka at once dispersed by words of power.

He had a harder task with the deathless serpent; it took three attempts to kill it, but after it had been cut in half and sand heaped up between the pieces it failed to recover, thanks possibly to further words of power.

Leaving the raft and climbing aboard the royal barge, Ptah the sorcerer opened the boxes one after the other on the sun-baked deck, his wife and son looking on. We are told that he read one of the two formulae inscribed in the Book, and so enchanted the earth and the heavens that he learned all their secrets; he read the second and he saw the sun rising in the heavens with his company of gods, and other fearful mysteries. His wife Ahura then read the Book and learned everything that her husband had seen.

It is a pity that the original papyrus does not give us details of these tremendous happenings; we are merely informed that Ptah-nefer-ka copied the writings upon a new piece of papyrus, covered it with a secret incense, dissolved it in water and drank it, thereby physically absorbing all the knowledge contained in the great Book of Thoth.

Unknown to the sorcerer, his act was witnessed by Thoth

himself, who became enraged at the sight of a mortal man usurping the powers of the gods; this blasphemy merited the direst punishment, and the decree went forth that the family should never return to Memphis.

And so it came about that on the journey back, Ahura and Merhu fell overboard and were drowned. Later, when Ptah-nefer-ka was returning with the Book on another vessel, he too, was drowned.

In the eerie light of the tomb, the two brothers had stood horrified listening to the grim tale, but Setnau's courage had not failed him, and he refused to be diverted from his purpose of obtaining the Book of Thoth that lay radiating its shimmering beams.

He dared not steal the Book from the dead, but he insisted in gaining possession of it. The story now takes an even stranger turn; we are told that Ptah-nefer-ka offered to play Setnau a game of draughts, the winner to have the Book. Try as he may, the sorcerer failed to win, even by trying to cheat, so the Book became the property of Setnau, who at once sent his brother up to the surface to bring him his amulets and books of magical writings.

Certain acts of magic followed, and we are told that Setnau became transformed and flew up to heaven with the Book in his hand surrounded by a blinding light. In the blackness of the tomb, the sorcerer said to Ahura, "I will make him return this Book to me with a knife and a rod in his hand and a vessel of fire upon his head."

Setnau had further adventures, but the final upshot was that the king ordered him to return the Book to its rightful place in the tomb of Ptah-nefer-ka. Although the story has rather a tame ending, there are a few entertaining highlights, such as the wife and son of Ptah-nefer-ka coming to reside in his tomb, although they were buried at Coptos; the raft and figures of the workmen made real so that they could do the donkey work of recovering the nest of boxes, and the literary device of making the Book glow with a mysterious light.

The idea of secreting the Book of Thoth in a nest of boxes, each of different materials, is an attractive one; the late Sax Rohmer, the mystery-fiction writer in his fascinating story, 'The Brood of the Witch Queen' used this identical device to good effect.

Chapter 8

A FEW THOUGHTS ON THE ETHICS OF EGYPTOLOGY

I must confess that from an early age, indeed from when I initially became interested in Egyptology and saw mummies for the first time, I have always felt rather shocked at the idea of invading ancient graves, digging up their contents, unwrapping the mummies and putting them on general display to the public. Even at this late date, I find myself in the grips of an ever increasing sense of outrage when I read the report of laying bare the shrivelled and naked body of the young Tutankhamen, with pictures of it all in the popular press.

To what extent are we justified in carrying out this work? Has scientific curiosity finally triumphed over conscience and morality? In answering these questions, we find ourselves on tricky ground. Firstly, are the acts of desecration lessened by the amount of time which has elapsed since the bodies were buried; in other words, is it perfectly acceptable to unwrap and expose the body of Tutankhamen merely because he died about 1500 years before Christ?

I realise of course that the almost insatiable thirst of scientific curiosity is a powerful driving force; in order to enlarge our knowledge of Egyptology (or of any other science for that matter) it is necessary to see the available material with our own eyes, to be able to touch it, evaluate it, weigh it and subject it to the scrutiny of modern electron microscopes. But are we not, to some extent, on a par with the ancient tomb-robbers and despoilers, who broke into the sepulchres, heaved the lids from the sarcophagi, and ravaged and tore the mummies in their mad search for gold and jewels?

'Ah', some will say, 'we don't do things like that today. We approach the matter in a spirit of, shall we say, reverence. Our interests are mainly scientific; we have the burning desire to gather and disseminate our newly acquired knowledge of the ancient Egyptians/Incas/Chinese/Mongolians (or what have you) among the world's scholars.'

Nevertheless, archaeologists have done, and still do break into tombs in order to remove the valuable contents to some museum; even today, digs are being carried out in the hope that fresh tombs will be uncovered, and I for one, although still feeling that sense of outrage and desecration, will read the reports of their findings with rapt attention.

When I was little more than a boy, an affection for the ancient Egyptians was aroused in me through viewing their works of art, the papyri, monuments, and by reading about their strange religion. One day, I had the audacity to approach Sir E.W. Wallis Budge the great Egyptologist, was received kindly by him, and encouraged in my studies on the subject. Among many other activities in the field of Egyptology, he had been present at and had taken part in the unwrapping of many mummies, and although I found his descriptions fascinating, I could not rid myself of the repugnance I felt and still feel at the idea of stripping the dead.

Perhaps the last quarter of the nineteenth century was the hey-day of the modern tomb-robber, masquerading in the guise of the archaeologist; today, however, archaeological digs are strictly controlled, at least in Egypt, where the government issues permits and has first claim upon all antiquities uncovered by the picks of the archaeologists.

There is one country today, namely Russia, in which the preserved body of perhaps its most famous son is kept on permanent display; daily, the faithful file past the body of Lenin in his magnificent tomb in Moscow. This is not a mummy in the true sense, because we associate mummies with linen bandaging, and Lenin's body is not wrapped, but it is a fine example of the embalmer's art.

There is a world of difference, however, between showing the body of Lenin in high honour to his own people, and exposing the poor stripped, shrivelled members of Tutankhamen (and others), or photographs of them, to the gaze of the morbidly curious.

One of the greatest discoveries ever made and which was saved, in the greater part, from the hands of the looter and antiquity hunter occurred at Der El-Bahari in 1881. Ten years previously, an Arab who lived by selling Egyptian antiquities (to which he had no right) to tourists, stumbled upon a large tomb which was literally stacked with coffins, most of them bearing royal cartouches.

The man was well aware of the value in the antique markets of his precious find, but he was faced with the immediate problem of handling the coffins. He would have preferred to keep his glorious secret to himself, but there was no help for it — he had to have assistance.

He decided to reveal his secret to his two brothers and to one of his sons, and so, under cover of the nights, they proceeded to move the coffins, burst them open and to strip the mummies of the amulets made of precious metals, ushabti figures, papyri, scarabs and other small objects which could be safely hidden under their robes.

For years this illicit trade went on, the brothers selling historically priceless articles to various tourists, and growing, meanwhile, rich but careless. I say careless, for the brothers reckoned without the intelligence and determination of people like M. Mariette and M. Maspero, two distinguished Frenchmen, the first being the founder of the Egyptian Museum at Gizeh, and the second its brilliant Director.

In time, some of these beautiful objects turned up in European cities, and people began to wonder from whence they came, and if perhaps an important 'find' had been made that had not been announced. For example, a British officer obtained a

Book of the Dead written in hieratic script and belonging to the High Priest Pi-net-em, and showed it to M. Maspero; M. Mariette himself purchased at Suez a papyrus which had been drawn up for Queen Hent-taiu.

The two Frenchmen agreed that the matter should be investigated immediately, and at once M. Maspero set off for Upper Egypt. A little detective work was indicated, and he soon succeeded in unearthing the names of three of the Arabs' dealers. The trail led him to Thebes, and soon he managed to effect the arrest of one of the wanted men.

An official inquiry was ordered by the authorities, and the man was closely questioned over a long period; it was even suggested that he was tortured in order to make him tell from whence the gang had obtained the antiquities, but whether it is true or not, he absolutely denied having any knowledge of the matter.

After spending two months in prison, he was released; perhaps the authorities thought that this move might eventually bring the results they were seeking. At any rate, as soon as the man rejoined his partners in crime, they began at once to plan for the future, but as is usual in such matters, it is not long before thieves begin to fall out. They started to quarrel, and the one who had been released from prison began to suspect that the others, in order to save their skins, might turn King's evidence should they be arrested.

To forestall this, the man chose the lesser of the two evils and decided to go to the magistrate to confess his complicity in the affair, and to reveal the location of the secret tomb.

When his statement had been verified, a small expedition led by another distinguished Frenchman, M. Emile Brugsch, was sent to investigate the contents of that veritable Aladdin's Cave in the valley of Der El-Bahari. It is said that the pit that led to the tomb was about forty feet deep, and the passage, of varying levels, which led to it was over two hundred feet long. At the end of this passage was a square chamber with walls twenty-five feet in length which was found to be stacked with mummies, coffins, funerary furniture and boxes, Canopic Jars, bowls and vases.

A large team of men was assembled to carry out the work of removing all the objects from the chamber and to transport them over the river to Luxor. Even for the Egyptian workmen well used to the heat, manhandling the heavy coffins from the chamber with its stifling heat and unbreathable and foul air up the long passage to the surface in the July heat of the summer of 1881 was terrible work.

For fully forty-eight hours, M. Brugsch and an Egyptian official stood guard at the mouth of the pit watching everything brought out; when the chamber was declared to be empty, they could relax. Meanwhile, the coffins and other items had been put into boats and sent across the river, but it was nearly a fortnight before everything had been cleared. Finally, the whole collection was placed on an Egyptian Government steamer and taken to the Museum at Bulak.

So much material had been assembled, that it was found that the museum was not large enough to contain the great number of articles and it become necessary to build several extra rooms.

Not very long after a selection of the mummies had been suitably put on display, several of them began to emit unpleasant odours. M. Maspero directed that they should be unrolled from their bandages, and one, that of Queen Aahmes Nefertari, became so putrified and stank so badly that it had to be buried. Others started to decay also, so Maspero ordered the whole collection to be unrolled. Thus it was that the face of one of Egypt's greatest kings, Rameses II, was seen again by men after a lapse of three thousand years.

Sir Wallis Budge's verdict on the discovery of the royal mummies at Der El-Bahari was: 'It will ever be regretted by the Egyptologist that this remarkable collection of mummies was not discovered by some person who could have used for the benefit of scholars the precious information which this "find" would have yielded, before so many of its objects were scattered;

as it is, however, it would be difficult to over-estimate its historical value.'

A short article in a national newspaper (29th May 1973) gives us a description of the activities of two groups of present-day tomb robbers in Egypt. At a spot near Beni Suef, about one hundred miles from Cairo, practically the whole village was engaged in digging operations, searching for antiquities which they hoped to be able to sell on the illegal antique market. Men from another village joined in and a gun battle broke out between the rival groups in which one man was killed and two others wounded. According to the article, the battle was fought in the tomb of a 700 BC Pharaoh; his name is not mentioned, but one of the finds was the mummy and coffin of Prince Ba-Khai-Si. The stone coffin is said to weigh fifteen tons, but this would be the outer stone sarcophagus, not the actual shell containing the body. Officials from the Egyptian Government have now taken charge of the finds, so it is to be hoped that the objects which the thieves got away with can be recovered and join the other antiquities in the Cairo Museum in due course.

With this brief review of the deciphering of the Egyptian hieroglyphics and of the art of the scribe, we move on now to consider the scripts of the prehistoric and historic races in the neighbouring lands of Mesopotamia.

Chapter 9

BOOKS OF CLAY

In previous chapters the good fortune of the Egyptians to have at hand such an abundance of material for paper-making in the papyrus swamps and their enterprise in making such use of it has been remarked upon.

They were also rich in many kinds of stone, from various qualities of limestone and sandstone, to alabaster and the very hard red and black granites. Material for brick-making was also very plentiful.

The ancient peoples living in the basins of the Tigris and Euphrates rivers were not so fortunate; in their arid lands, no papyrus plants grew. Stone they certainly had, but their correspondence was scratched or impressed upon pieces of clay.

One of the most remarkable discoveries ever made in Egypt were the so-called Tell-el-Amarna Tablets. Some Arabs, living on the site of Akhenaten's city, Akhetaten (Horizon of the Aten, of Sun's Disc), had found a cache of over three hundred clay documents bearing wedge-shaped markings, had cut them up, and were hawking them to dealers and tourists.

Some people, dealers in Egyptian curios and antiques bought them; a few scholars looked at them and pronounced them to be forgeries. They must be fakes — how could Babylonian tablets possibly be found in Egypt? they asked.

A scholar from the Berlin Museum saw some of them however, and realised the importance of the find; there began almost at once a furious search for the rest of the tablets. These documents which had suddenly become so important were written about 1500 BC in Akkadian, a cuneiform script, and represented official diplomatic correspondence between the kings of Egypt and the rulers of Assyria, Asia Minor, Babylonia and Syria. They supplied entirely new information concerning political relations and proved that important trade existed between the nations.

Facts also came to light regarding treaties and alliances and, for the first time, they gave historians the names of Artatama, Artashumara and Tushratta, kings of Mitanni and Karaduniyash.

The earliest dwellers in the valleys of the Euphrates were a people known as Sumerians; they too felt the need to record events and transactions in a more or less permanent form and were among the first to use tablets of clay upon which they scratched their picture-symbols. Examples of these tablets are on view in the British Museum and elsewhere and of particular interest are those found in the recent past at Uruk in Southern Mesopotamia; several thousand were uncovered and provide a strong clue to the development of writing in its earliest stages.

A clay tablet inscribed with a part of the Babylonian story of the Creation. About 700 BC.

Upon close inspection it will be seen that the picture word-signs are very crudely drawn, but it should be remembered that clay is not the ideal material for drawing upon. The earliest tablets, dating from about 3000 BC are limited to the expression of numbers, objects and personal names. It is rather disappointing to report that the Uruk tablets and inscriptions remain, as yet, a mystery.

As time went on, the writing of the Sumerian scribes underwent changes; circles, curves and arcs are not easily made upon clay, especially if the message had to be hurriedly recorded by the scribe. The writing became angular; for instance, he would express a circle by means of a few separate strokes of his drawing stick or stylus, and due to natural causes and pressure, a little nick would appear at the beginning of each stroke. And so was born cuneiform writing.

There is hardly the need to remind the reader that the same thing happened with the Egyptian scribes; the use of hieratic was a faster way to fill the page than writing the beautiful but cumbersome hieroglyphs.

A cuneiform inscription, when done well, looks very fine and this opinion was shared by the scribes and priests of Sumeria and of the other races that followed them, for this writing was carved upon wood, stone and metal.

A note on the technique of Cuneiform writing

All that was required was a substance on which to write, and a tool. Cuneiform was written, as far as available evidence shows, in the following ways:

(a)   on clay with a reed stylus. This was the commonest material to hand and the obvious choice. Afterwards, the tablets were sun-dried or baked. The stylus was a straight piece of stick, reed, bone or metal. On some monuments, Assyrian scribes are shown holding the stylus in a closed fist but it is likely that this method would have led to faulty and inaccurate signs since the natural sensitivity of the 'writing position' would have been lost.

(b)   on stone with a chisel, upon monuments, reliefs, statues, etc. In this case, the work would not be done by a scribe but by a specialised worker who would follow the text draft.

(c)   upon metal, using a hard chisel.

(d)   upon wax with a metal point. Texts on wooden boards coated with beeswax have been found, but only at Nimrud.

(e)   on glazed terracotta with a brush. This is the only case where cuneiform was actually painted and not impressed or engraved and any examples extant of this type are late Assyrian.

The stylus was cut in such a way as to enable the scribe to form the signs by pressing the end of it into the soft clay.

Wedges could be impressed in the following directions:

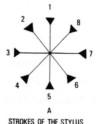

5, 6, 7 and 8 were seldom used for practical reasons, 1, 2, 3 and 4 eventually remaining the only wedges in use, 4 being relatively rare.

A

STROKES OF THE STYLUS

By slightly altering the position of the stylus, the wedges could be made shorter or longer, while two more wedges could be made by changing the position still further. Thus, in short, the scribe had the following double row of wedges at his disposal:

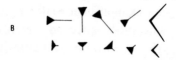

B

and these he could combine in any of the signs making up the cuneiform script. Cuneiform is written from left to right. Earlier, it was written from top to bottom in columns running from right to left. During cuneiform development, the tablets were turned ninety degrees to the left, the top-to-bottom, right to left *column* becoming left to right top to bottom *lines.*

The Assyrians had about five hundred and seventy signs,

although only about three hundred of these were in common use, and there was constant progress towards simplification of the signs, reducing the number of wedges used.

Who were the users of cuneiform script? The first, as we have seen, were the Sumerians. As time progressed, Semitic people adopted the Sumerian script, together with their religious language, and also borrowed from Sumerian literature.

Next, the Akkadians, the people of Babylonia and Assyria. Here, there were six main periods in the long development of cuneiform writing, as follows:

1 Early Akkadian
2 Early Babylonian
3 Kassite
4 Assyrian
5 Neo-Babylonian
6 A revival, and the end of cuneiform writing, 3rd century BC to the 1st century AD.

As well as the foregoing, other people took over this method of writing: the Elamites, Hittites, Mitanni, Huuri, Luwi, Balai, Urartu, and the Persians.

Cuneiform lingered on into the Christian era, being kept alive by priests, lawyers and astronomers. Aramaic took its place in business and private correspondence.

Archaeology is indebted to Sir Henry Rawlinson for his outstanding achievement in deciphering the trilingual cuneiform scripts, and to the painstaking work of Grotefend and many others who preceded him. At the end of the eighteenth century, not a word of cuneiform could be read with any certainty; by the end of the nineteenth, the contents of thousands of lengthy records of great empires were recovered for the use of modern scholars.

The deciphering of Hittite 'hieroglyphic' writing was achieved only in the 1930s by Helmut Bossert of Germany; Emil Forrer of Switzerland; Bedrich Hrozny of Czechoslovakia; Piero Meriggi of Italy and I. Gelb of the United States, but very little progress was made, and none at all on the level of Sumerian or Ancient Egyptian. It was in use from Anatolia to Northern Syria from about 1500 BC to 700 BC, and appeared in both hieroglyphic and cursive forms. The ancient Elamite script, (still undeciphered) first appeared at Susa, the capital of ancient Elam. It was inscribed on clay tablets, stone stele and seals.

I. Gelb is of the opinion that the oldest of the oriental systems of writing is the Sumerian, and that it dates from around 3100 BC. The main principles of it may have spread from Mesopotamia eastward, to the neighbouring Proto-Elamites, and then by way of the latter to the Proto-Indians in the valley of the Indus.

Regarding Proto-Indic inscriptions, about two hundred and fifty assorted signs have been found on seals, pottery and copper tablets. The writing of another ancient people, the Cretans, shows development from hieroglyphic form to linear. We use the term 'hieroglyphic' here merely to indicate the use of pictograms — picture-words.

Some readers may wish to put a question at this point. They may well ask, what about Chinese; isn't that an ancient writing?

It certainly is, but the striking fact about Chinese is that it was not necessary to decipher it in modern times, because it's development stages passed from generation to generation. The Chinese system of writing first appeared about the middle of the second millenium BC, during the Shang dynasty and was reorganised and standardised in about 212 BC by Li Ssu who was Emperor Ch'in Shih Hwang Ti's Prime Minister.

The evolution from pictograms to full cuneiform

It is fascinating to study the way in which many of the cuneiform characters can be traced back, by means of older forms, to the original picture-words. Let us begin with 'ox' ⊨ ⟩⧏ 'alpu'. This stemmed from hieratic Babylonian, ⫪⟩ which in Linear Babylonian is ⇒. If the sign is turned 90° to the right, it is recognisable as the head and horns of an ox. It should be noted that this does not differ greatly from ⟨, in which the Phoenicians saw the likeness of an ox's head (aleph), and which has given us the name of our alphabet.

The sign for 'fish' is as easy to trace as the previous example. In the Assyrian cuneiform we find 𐎟 (kha)=fish; the likeness has almost disappeared, but it can be recognised if we go to archaic Babylonian, in which the form of the character is ⟫⟨. A still older form is ⟫◁, while in the linear Babylonian we have ⟨⟫⟪.

Here is an example by which we can see the manner in which compound characters arose from combinations of simple forms. In this case, the ideogram employed to denote the city of Nineveh was ⟫𐎟⟨|. The archaic form of this is ⟫◱⟩=the picture of a house enclosing the ideogram for 'fish'. This is an interesting example of ancient place-naming; it indicates that the grand city of Nineveh was, at first, merely a collection of fishermen's huts. A parallel might be found in the London district called Whitechapel: as far as I know, there is no white chapel there now, but clearly, in olden times, a white church may have been the most important building in the place.

In the accompanying tables showing the development from drawings to advanced cuneiform, it will be seen to be far from clear how the Neo-Assyrians and Neo-Babylonians arrived at their final choice of signs; it is plain, however, that in every case economy of line had been their aim.

DEVELOPMENT OF CUNEIFORM SCRIPT

PICTOGRAPHS			CLASSICAL SUMERIAN		OLD AKKADIAN 2200 B.C.	OLD ASSYRIAN 1900 B.C.	OLD BABYLONIAN 1700 B.C.	NEO ASSYRIAN 700 B.C.	NEO BABYLONIAN 600 B.C.	MEANING
URUK VERTICAL	3100 B.C. TURNED 90°	JEMDAT NASR	LINE	CUNEIFORM						
										OX
										STREAM SEED SON
										PUDENDUM MULIEBRE
										STAR HEAVEN GOD
										BIRD
										HEAD
										MAN
										PLOUGH
										DONKEY
										GRAIN
										SUN DAY LIGHT
										FISH
										HOUSE

Chapter 10

The birth and development of Assyriology took place roughly between the middle of the nineteenth century and the beginning of the twentieth century, since which time new discoveries have been made, and much new material added to the world's knowledge.

As Champollion with his great gifts was the main decipherer of ancient Egyptian writing, so an Englishman, Sir Henry Rawlinson, is entitled to be styled the 'Father of Assyriology'. It was he who first copied down, deciphered, and translated the famous trilingual inscriptions of Darius the Great on the Rock of Behistun; he was Director of Excavations in Mesopotamia for the Trustees of the British Museum between 1846 and 1855, and was Editor-in-Chief of the five volumes of the Cuneiform Inscriptions of Western Asia, which were published between 1856 and 1884.

It will not be out of place, I think, to give the reader some facts about this remarkable man. He was a great scholar and linguist; he was also an athlete and a fine horseman, and he possessed the will and determination to finish anything he had once begun.

He was born at Chadlington Park in Oxfordshire in 1810, and when at school in Ealing in London, he devoted much extra time to the study of the Greek and Latin historians. When he was sixteen he secured a position with the Honourable East India Company and arrived in India in 1827. Not content merely to carry out his duties and to enjoy himself in his spare time, he studied Persian, Arabic and Hindustani with such effect that by the next year he was made interpreter and paymaster to the 1st Bombay Grenadiers.

He had a great gift for learning oriental languages and was able to quote by heart long passages from the great Persian poets, an ability which, in later life (1875), brought an appointment from the British Government for him to meet the Shah of Persia to discuss matters of political importance in the Shah's own language.

Rawlinson served the Regiment for five years, afterwards (1833) being employed on special duties with Intelligence. In 1835 he was appointed to act as Military Adviser to the Shah's brother in Kirmanshah. While he was on his way there he heard about the existence of some mysterious cuneiform inscriptions on a rocky slope of Mount Elvend. When time allowed, he rode to the place and copied them down. These inscriptions formed the basic material from which he extracted the names of Darius and Xerxes; this work prepared him, so to speak, for his later discoveries in the Persian cuneiform inscriptions.

No sooner had he arrived at Kirmanshah when he was told about a large inscription with human figures carved in relief high up on the Rock of Behistun. This was thrilling news, and he made frequent visits to the Rock during the summer and autumn of 1835.

During the nineteenth century, and earlier of course, many other people had seen these inscriptions and had endeavoured to copy them with the aid of small telescopes or field-glasses, but Rawlinson, being young and athletic, climbed the Rock and managed to reach the ledge which projected just below the inscriptions without the help of ladders or ropes. When one considers that the text is cut into the almost vertical surface of the solid rock five hundred feet above the ground, Rawlinson's first effort was no mean feat.

During the next two years he continued to copy down sections of the inscriptions whenever he could be spared from his duties. It should be realized that the task was no minor matter, for besides there being hundreds of lines of text to copy, all of it was in three languages. At the end of 1837 Rawlinson had taken down two hundred lines from the Persian text and he returned to Baghdad with the material, where he worked upon it for nearly a year.

Now an unfortunate occurrence interrupted his studies — in 1839 the Afghan War began and he was appointed Political Agent in Kandahar. He took part in a battle near Kandahar in which he led a troop of Persian cavalrymen, trained by himself, and assisted at the capture of Ghazni, all with complete success. With the close of the war his military career ended, for he was impatient to get back to the study of his inscriptions.

The opportunity occurred with the retirement of Colonel Taylor, the Political Agent in Turkish Arabia, when Rawlinson was appointed to succeed him (1843). He took up his new post in Baghdad and in the following year he made plans to tackle the inscriptions in earnest.

This time, however, he had some skilled help in the persons of a Mr Hester and Captain Felix Jones, RN, whose assistance enabled him to make exact copies of the Persian and Susian Versions from the face of the great Rock.

Although ladders and ropes were to hand on this occasion, the task was one of great difficulty needing a head for heights, steady nerves and iron determination. It could have been no easy task either for the original stone-cutters despite the fact that they would have been provided with scaffolding and a small army of labourers with ropes and ladders.

Rawlinson's own account of the way he mastered the difficulties is interesting. Upon reaching the recess containing the Persian text he at once saw the need for ladders in order to examine the upper part of the tablet but, even with their use, there was great risk because the foot-ledge was so narrow (no more than two feet wide) that with a ladder long enough to reach the inscriptions, sufficient angle could not be obtained to allow a man to climb.

On the other hand, if a shorter ladder was used, the upper

markings could only be copied if he stood upon the top step — a frightful prospect! But there was no other choice left to him, so he edged his way to the topmost step, and with no other support than steadying his body against the rock with his left arm while his left hand held the notebook, he began to copy down the upper inscriptions, and in his own words, 'the interest of the occupation entirely did away with any sense of danger.'

To reach the recess which contains the Scythic translation of the record of Darius was a task of even greater danger and difficulty; on the left side of the recess only was there any kind of foot-ledge; on the right, the face of the rock presented a sheer precipice, and Rawlinson had to think of some way to bridge it.

If his ladders had been long enough for this particular operation, a bridge could have been made, but only with difficulty.

His first attempt to cross the chasm failed and might have been fatal, because having shortened his only ladder in order to obtain sufficient angle for copying the Persian scripts, he found, when laying it across to the recess in order to reach the Scythic part, that it was not long enough to lie flat on the foot-ledge beyond.

Only one side of the ladder would reach the nearest point of the ledge; any attempt to cross over would have caused it to tilt, with fatal consequences. There was only one thing to do: stand the ladder on its edge with its upper length resting firmly on the rock at its two ends and its lower hanging in space!

He now proposed to cross by walking on the lower length while holding on to the upper length with his hands in crab-like fashion.

What happened next would have been uproariously funny if it had not been near-tragic. Rawlinson writes, 'If the ladder had been a compact article, this manner of crossing, although far from comfortable, would have been practicable, but the Persians merely fit in the bars of their ladders without clenching them outside, and I had hardly begun to cross over when the vertical pressure forced the bars out of their sockets . . . .'

Several bars and the lower side of the ladder parted company and went crashing down five hundred feet to the ground. Rawlinson, desperately hanging on to the upper length, was rescued by his companions, and regained the Persian recess. He did not attempt another crossing until he had made a more substantial 'bridge'.

All was not lost however; he had won his copies of the Persian and Scythic (Susian) Versions. He returned to Baghdad to study the results of the adventure; his present equipment had not been sufficient to have enabled him to obtain the Babylonian Version as well. In 1847 he returned once more to the Rock to obtain his copy of this latter set of inscriptions and, upon arrival, at once saw that its position on the Rock would rule out his previous method, copying out by hand on sheets of paper.

If Rawlinson had lived in our times, his task would have presented no difficulty whatever; given the use of a small helicopter and modern photographic equipment, the survey would have taken merely a few hours. However, he did not, and he had to gain his knowledge the hard way. He tells us that the Babylonian section was even more difficult to reach than either the Susian or Persian tablets. It could have been copied with the help of a good telescope from below, but he was anxious to obtain a cast, yet found it beyond his powers to attempt to climb to the spot. Native goat-herders had assured him that the place was quite unapproachable.

Hanging about Rawlinson's camp was a young Kurdish boy who seemed keen to make himself useful. Having picked up the gist of Rawlinson's problem, he volunteered to try to reach the spot and to carry out whatever he was asked to do. Anxiously watched by the whole party of adults, the boy, nimble and as light as a feather, began the ascent. Having safely approached the spot, his next act was to press himself up a cleft in the rock a short distance from the main obstacle, a projecting mass of stone. Working himself up further, he drove a wooden peg hard into a cleft, tied a rope to it, then attempted to swing himself across to another cleft several yards away. He did not succeed, because of the overhanging rock, but he was not put off, although for a few moments he swung twirling about like a puppet on a string.

There only remained one way for him to get across, and that was by hanging on by his fingers and toes to every slight dent in the perpendicular face. The plucky boy moved across a distance of over twenty feet like a fly on the wall. Everybody breathed again as he reached the second substantial cleft to comparative safety, and drove in another wooden peg. With the rope he had brought, he managed to swing himself over the projecting rock.

With a short light ladder, he made a swinging seat, after the style of a painter's cradle, and under Rawlinson's directions he made paper casts of the Babylonian inscriptions. No one in history, except the original craftsmen, had been so close to the trilingual inscriptions, over five hundred feet above the ground, as Rawlinson and his assistants.

At this point, the Kurdish boy leaves the pages of history, but it is to be hoped that he was well rewarded for his work.

What happened to the paper casts that had been obtained by so much honest effort? They were brought to London and exhibited by Rawlinson in the rooms of various learned societies before whom he lectured, and, later, he presented them to the Trustees of the British Museum. Eventually, they were stored for some years behind the great man-headed bull in the Assyrian Gallery where they suffered by being handled by scholars and by the inroads of mice.

In the 1890s, there was still great interest being shown in the subject of Assyriology, and the Trustees decided to publish a *Corpus* of cuneiform inscriptions. When the paper casts were brought into the open and examined, many were seen to be hopelessly damaged while others were missing. No new work on the subject could be considered until new material was assembled.

It happened that in 1904, a scholar from the Department of

Egyptian and Assyrian Antiquities, L.W. King, was excavating at Kuyunjik, the modern Nineveh. One day he received instructions to go to the Rock of Behistun, recollect all the texts, take measurements and procure photographs. He had a trustworthy colleague and the services of a gang of native workers to help him reach the inscriptions. It was a task demanding skill and resourcefulness; in this case he decided to use cradles suspended from above the great inscription.

He found a better route up the mountain which led him to a rocky ledge two hundred feet above the site. Here, the workers drove steel crowbars into cracks in the rock and from these, ropes were lowered to the required levels and cradles fixed to them. The cradles were lowered or raised by the natives at a signal so that the next section could be copied. The results of King's work and that of his companion can still be read in the pages of *The Sculptures and Inscriptions of Darius the Great on the Rock of Behistun in Persia*, which was published in 1907.

Readers should not be discouraged by the title of the volume, which contains the complete texts of the Persian, Susian and Babylonian cuneiform scripts, with translations, and many photographs.

Chapter 11

Many of the earlier travellers to Persia had seen the strange arrow-head writing on various monuments and tombs, and had regarded it as part of the ornamentation, while others had guessed the marks to be writing of some kind.

One traveller, however, Karsten Niebuhr (1733-1815) was rather more curious than the rest. He was the first man to copy down some of the characters with any accuracy, recognise that the inscriptions were in three languages, and was also the first to show that they were to read from left to right. He drew up an 'alphabet' of 42 characters, and of these, 32 are accepted as being correct. He was in error on nine of the others, and he failed to guess the meaning of the oblique sign for dividing words.

He published the result of his work on the inscriptions in his *Voyage* in 1780 which fired the interest of scholars everwhere; if he had failed to do so, it is quite likely that the decipherment of the cuneiform inscriptions would have been deferred for many generations. Neibuhr made his copies among the Takht-i-Jamshid ruins which lie about 40 miles north-east of Shiraz. The word means 'Throne of Jamshid' and the ruins are the remains of some once-splendid palaces near the site of a great city built by Darius I and Xerxes.

The first to take up Niebuhr's torch was Olaus Tychsen (1734-1813), a Hebrew scholar; but his studies did not take him very far although a few of his phonetic values proved to be correct.

The circle was widening, and now another scholar, F.C. Munter (1761-1830) tried his hand at deciphering the Persian

A brick stamped with the name and titles of Nebuchadnezzar II, King of Babylon, and those of his father, Nabopolassar. 604–605 BC.

cuneiform inscriptions after reading Niebuhr's book. He proved that they belonged to the period of the Achaemenian dynasties, and he believed that the first form of the writing (Persian) was alphabetic; the second, (Susian) syllabic, and the third (Babylonian) ideographic. He was correct in recognising the diagonal wedge as a word-divider.

He too was an inspired guesser, and observed that one group of seven signs was frequently repeated; this led him (and others) to assume that these represented the name of a king. Later, he changed his opinion and thought that after all they may have formed a title – perhaps 'King of Kings' and that the name preceding this group must be the name of a king. These signs, which read *Kh-Sha-A-Ya-Th-I-Ya,* mean 'King'; it could be said with reason that this sound is not too far removed from 'Kaiser' or Caesar.

On firmer ground was G.F. Grotefend (1775-1853), a scholar with the type of mind which delighted in all kinds of puzzles. He came across the texts of Niebuhr and Munter and became fascinated with the problem, but not being an orientalist he relied solely upon his powers of deduction. He became convinced that the inscriptions copied down by Niebuhr contained the names of two kings, and that the seven signs did actually mean 'King of Kings'. But who were the two kings? Cyrus, or Cambyses? This could not be, for if they were, both names would begin with the same sign-letter.

Finally he deduced that one of the inscriptions possessed the value of 'Hystaspes' and decided the king was Darius; working on the same lines he concluded that the second king was Xerxes. He was proved to be right, but after these successes he became bogged down in the dangerous marshes of oriental languages, contributing little of value, although he continued to believe in his own powers – that he was the one man able to decipher the mass of new material that was even then coming to light.

Many other European scholars contributed something of value to the long process of deciphering the cuneiform inscriptions, for example Christian Rask (1787-1832), Eugene Burnouf (1801-1852) and Christian Lassen (1800-1876); each studied the findings of the others, sometimes gaining a letter here or a clearer meaning there. Lassen examined the inscriptions published by his contemporaries and found one by Niebuhr containing a mention of twenty-four proper names. After some hard thinking he drew up an 'alphabet' of twenty-three letters, to which he gave correct phonetic values and of the twenty-four names, he managed to identify nineteen.

One of the brightest stars in the history of Assyriology was a young man, Eugene Stanislaus Jaquet (1811-1837), who devoted his short life to the study of cuneiform writing, and wrote a brilliant essay on Cuneiform Decipherment which was universally acclaimed.

He had hardly left school when he plunged into the vigorous study of several oriental languages; he corresponded with other European scholars and added six correct values to the Persian alphabet, arriving at his results quite independently. He had two great loves; one was his widowed mother, and the other his passionate thirst for knowledge. In his feverish desire to learn more and to add to the total of Assyrian knowledge, he sacrificed his health. When he was only twenty-four he contracted a fatal disease; during the last three years of his life, he struggled, in the face of much suffering, to complete his studies. He died at his desk, surrounded by his papers, manuscripts and books. He will always be remembered for his contributions to the decipherment of the cuneiform inscriptions, for his gallant spirit and for the single-mindedness he displayed towards his work.

Among all those who worked at the decipherment of the inscriptions, there was none to match Rawlinson. With perfect justice, he has been called the 'Father of Assyriology', and yet, in his day, he had many detractors, especially among the Europeans. Indeed, in some works his name is hardly mentioned. Some even said that he cribbed from Grotefend, but these allegations have no substance, and Rawlinson's decipherment of the inscriptions from both Mount Elvend and the Rock of Behistun are monuments to his scholarship and integrity.

Rawlinson, like Grotefend, had a gift for solving problems and puzzles but, in his case, this gift was backed up by an excellent classical education. He saw that the two inscriptions from Elvend were practically identical and deduced that they contained proper names. From his knowledge of the classics, he applied to them the royal names of Hystaspes, Darius, and Xerxes and found that he was correct. These names, however, produced only thirteen characters, which he assumed to be alphabetic; from his reading, when still a youth, of the works of Herodotus, Rawlinson remembered that the great Xerxes, in his speech to Artabanus made known his family line, saying that he was the son of Darius, the son of Hystaspes, the son of Arsames, the son of Ariaramnes, the son of Teispes, the son of Cyrus, the son of Cambyses, the son of Teispes, the son of Achaemenes.

Although it seemed obvious to him that there were only three royal names in the Mount Elvend inscriptions, it was worth looking again at the Behistun records to see whether they would provide more. If they could, he thought, and if he could identify the groups, the Greek forms of the names as they appeared in Herodotus would help him to put values on the characters from Behistun.

To his great joy, this idea bore fruit; here are just four of the groups with the results he arrived at, together with his reasoning:

Take number 1 first. Rawlinson already knew the values of the first four signs, A.R.SH.A., these formed part of the Greek Arsames; therefore he thought, he last sign must be M − this gave him ARSAM.

Again, in number 2, he was aware of the values of all the signs except one, the first. Deducing this to be H, he wrote down this group as KH.A.M.N.I.SH.I.Y.A., the 'Achaemenian' of Herodotus. This 'H', by the way, is the hard-sounding H like the *ch* in the Scottish 'loch'.

In the third group he also knew all of the values except that of the last one − A.R.I.Y.A.R.M., which represented the Greek

112

Ariaramnes, so the last sign must be an N.

With the last group Rawlinson had no trouble at all — he could read P.A.R.SA.I.YA., which is the name PERSIA.

Thus encouraged, he worked his way through the Behistun inscriptions and obtained the values of a great many more letters, for example:

From Artavardiya he extracted	𝌆	= D
From Athura (Assyria) he extracted ..	𝌆	= TH
From Atrina he extracted	𝌆	= TR
From Auramazda he extracted	𝌆	= Z
From Babirush (Babylon) he extracted	𝌆	= B
and	𝌆	= R
From Bagabigna he extracted	𝌆	= G
From Kabujiya (Cambyses) he extracted	𝌆	= J
From Katpatuka he extracted	𝌆	= K
and	𝌆	= T before U
From Chorasmia he extracted	𝌆	= M
From Kurush (Cyrus) he extracted ..	𝌆	= K
From Mudraya (Egypt) he extracted ..	𝌆	= M before U
From Uvaja he extracted	𝌆	= J before A

A most determined person, Rawlinson worked solidly at his enormous and tedious task, enlarging his alphabet day by day, even returning to Kirmanshah to copy down more signs from the great inscription. For a whole year (1837) he worked at his texts, and was finally able to make a good translation of the first two paragraphs from the Behistun inscription. He sent this, with his notes, to the Royal Asiatic Society in London, where on the advice of the Assistant Secretary, a copy of the work was sent to the Société Asiatique in Paris. The members of that society thought so highly of Rawlinson's papers that they promptly elected him an Honorary Member.

Let there be no mistake made about the work of Rawlinson in the field of Assyriology. It was he who founded the science of Assyriology, and it was established solely by the Trustees of the British Museum. He was the first man to ascend the Rock of Behistun and to copy, *decipher* and *translate* the huge inscription in three languages carved upon it by the order of Darius the Great. He was the Director of Excavations in Mesopotamia for the Trustees between 1846 and 1855; for forty years he was the director of all matters connected with cuneiform writing, and his work on the Semitic texts from the Neneveh tablets alone gives him the right to be called the 'Father of Assyriology'.

And yet, there were people, both in Britain and on the Continent, who asserted that Rawlinson never left the ground, but copied the inscriptions with the aid of a small telescope. Others attempted to prove that the decipherment and translations were carried out by Continental scholars, Grotefend, Burnouf, Rask, Lassen and so on, and alleged that Rawlinson owed his triumph to their researches.

To those readers who meet similar misstatements in their future reading I would recommend the following books: *The Rise and Progress of Assyriology* by Sir E.A. Wallis Budge, Kt, and *The Discovery and Decipherment of the Trilingual Cuneiform Inscriptions* by Arthur John Booth, M.A. In the pages of these two volumes the reader will be able to investigate in depth the colossal work of scholarship carried out by Rawlinson, and to judge the evidence of the originality of his work.

As previously indicated, the inscriptions on the sheer face of the Rock of Behistun were executed in three languages — Old Persian, Susian and Babylonian. Nobody could fail to admire Rawlinson for his perseverence and sheer physical determination in the attainment of his goal — the complete decipherment and translation of the languages on the Rock.

He published his translation of the Susian Version in 1845. From his high perch he had seen that the inscriptions were in a very poor state of preservation due to the ravages of wind and rain, but his knowledge was so wide and his instincts so sure that he was able to supply the meanings of broken or missing signs.

Rawlinson visited the Rock again in 1847 to copy the Babylonian Version, afterwards returning to Baghdad to begin the decipherment of the fresh harvest of signs. To help himself with the translation he found it necessary to resume his studies of Hebrew and Syriac.

It would be tedious to place before the reader everything that transpired during the decipherment and publication of the cuneiform texts, such as the acrimonious bickering that raged among scholars and interested parties everywhere. For instance, some writers, hoping to rob Rawlinson of the credit due to him, asserted that it was entirely owing to the work of Grotefend that we are able to understand the meaning of the inscriptions; most of us, however, are content to be guided by the records of the British Museum.

Credit is due to Grotefend on a number of points; he managed to translate the names of Hystaspes, Darius and Xerxes and obtained the correct values of eight characters, but he failed in recognising that Babylonian was a Semitic language. Inspired guessing is all very well, but Grotefend lacked the knowledge of the oriental languages that are so necessary in work of this kind.

The Sumerians, the people who inhabited the valleys of the Euphrates and Tigris, were not a Semitic race. The linear writing they invented was gradually developed through the centuries by others until it arrived at its final form at the time of the Christian era, that is to say, using the most economical amount of strokes per character.

It was while Rawlinson was labouring at his translations that some entirely new inscriptions were sent to him from Southern Babylon in another and quite different language. Shortly after, a great number of tablets were discovered, and investigations indicated that these inscriptions were the work of ancient Sumerian scribes and that the language belonged to the Turanian family. To begin with, the new language was given the name of 'Akkadian', but it is known today as Sumerian.

Sumerian clay tablets inscribed with pictographs, which preceded the cuneiform script. Jemdet Nasr Period.

The signs consist of little line drawings somewhat after the style of the early Egyptian hieroglyphs, but far cruder; these characters preceded the use of the wedge-shaped writing. The illustration shows how the little drawings developed into the full-blooded cuneiform script which owed its typical appearance to the use of the stylus.

It did not take the scholars very long to come to the conclusion that cuneiform writing stemmed from the Sumerian linear script. Moreover, as they delved deeper into the matter, they discovered that not only the writing but also the religion and literature of later times had descended from that Turanian race who had inhabited the fertile areas of the two rivers. There seemed to be no doubt that these people were the forerunners of civilisation in Western Asia, and it was from them that the Semitic peoples who came to the valleys in later times acquired their notions of law, the basis of their religious beliefs, legends and literature.

As work proceeded, the immense antiquity of the Sumerian civilisation was made manifest; it appeared that the beginnings of Sumerian history dated back as far as 6000 BC. The British Museum inclined to an even earlier period, suggesting a figure of 8000 BC.

While the majority of British and European scholars, convinced at the evidence brought to light, accepted the existence of Sumerian, the non-Semitic language spoken and written by the race who lived in Babylonia long before the arrival of new populations, there were some, among them noted French scholars such as M. Renan and J. Halévy, who violently disagreed. Halévy tried to prove that Sumerian was not a language at all, but merely an ideographical system of writing which the Assyrians had invented; he also tried to prove that no Turanian people had ever existed in Babylonia, and if Sumerian was a language, it did not belong to the Turanian family anyway.

M. Renan, also unconvinced, could not bring himself to believe that the ancient Semitic people worshipped several gods, instead of one; he overlooked the fact that the Assyrian Galleries in the Louvre began to be crowded with images of strange pagan gods made of burnt clay. He too could not accept the fact that the Turanian people could really be the founders of human culture in Western Asia.

It could be thought that archaeology ranked among the most peaceful of sciences, but in this case it was not so; the arguments and correspondence between scholars and writers were exceedingly long-drawn and bitter, but in the end, nobody could argue with the evidence history had submitted for investigation.

Let us bring the argument nearer home for the moment; could it be that our Christian beliefs of today are merely pale, distorted reflections, compounded form ancient Egyptian and Hebraic myths which perhaps originated in the immensely antique legends and myths of the Sumerians?

In an earlier chapter the similarity between certain aspects of the Christian faith and that of ancient Egypt was indicated — how the Sun-god Ra was the Creator of all things, and how Osiris, his only son, was murdered by Set, rose from the dead, and became the absolute symbol of the Resurrection to the Ancient Egyptians who planted all their hopes for everlasting life upon this event. Many people today would reject this proposition outright as being almost blasphemous; they could be said to be of the same school of thought as Halévy and Renan.

History itself is a history of man's borrowing, adaptation and modification of ideas. The ancient Egyptians practised circumcision of boys and girls, and on certain days, no flame was allowed to burn in a house. The Hebrews adopted the latter custom, and only circumcised young males. These ancient customs are kept to this day among Jewish people.

We have all borrowed from each other; our own alphabet, as we have seen, can be traced back into the very ancient past; we have cheerfully adopted the old Nordic names for the days of the week, while on the Continent they use the names of the Roman gods. Our surgeons, doctors, pharmacists, biologists and horticulturists use Latin and some Greek, while the Japanese adopted the Chinese system of writing.

It would appear that the family of Man on earth is more closely knit than we sometimes realise.

The British Museum and Assyriologists everywhere owe a debt of gratitude to a remarkable man for his skill in cleaning, repairing and preserving the thousands of seals, tablets and other antiquities that were given into his care. He was Robert Walpole Ready (1811-1903); he entered the service of the Museum in 1858, and began to apply his skills on some of the tablets from Mesopotamia. He had a good working knowledge of practical chemistry, and to aid him in his work, he invented many secret processes by which he was able to restore antiquities thought by experts to be beyond saving.

Large pieces of sculpture, bas-reliefs, etc. sent from Mesopotamia had arrived safely packed in mats and iron-bound wooden cases, but thousands of clay tablets bearing cuneiform scripts had been sent off to England tied up loosely in straw baskets which had been dumped in rough boxes. The tablets were covered in dust and earth which was carefully brushed off, but some had strange patches of a crystalline substance adhering to them. None of the officials at the Museum had any idea how to remove the deposits, and their various attempts always ended in disaster, the tablets crumbling in their hands.

A certain repairer employed by the Museum was allowed to try out some of his own ideas, such as baking some of the unbaked tablets from Nineveh, or immersing them in a special solution of his own, but the result was the same in both cases — in the first, the surfaces flaked off and fell into dust, and in the second, the tablets disintegrated in the liquid. After this, nothing was done until Mr Ready joined the staff, paid on an hourly basis. It is worth recording that the job, although considered a permanent one, carried no pension, and his pay was very meagre. One would have thought that in view of his wonderful services to Assyriology the officials could have seen their way to organising a pension for him, or failing that, to pay him a salary commensurate with his skill and enterprise.

One of Ready's triumphs was the saving of many of the shallow pottery bowls from Babylon which were used for divining. They had not been in England very long when a strange thing happened to them. Long silky white filaments began to shoot out from their surfaces, destroying the Syriac inscriptions on their inside faces. Other people had tried to save the bowls by painting them with varnish or other substances, but the result was always failure.

Ready subjected the filaments to chemical analysis and found them to be composed of sodium. His method was to extract the salt, which he did by immersing the bowls in cool distilled water for about a week. To his joy, the feathery growths had ceased to bloom, and the inscriptions were saved.

Among other valuable work carried out by Ready for the British Museum was a method of making plaster impressions from the stone cylinders the Assyrians, Babylonians, Persians and others used as seals for impressing on clay 'documents'. His work can be seen to this day in the Assyrian Galleries of the British Museum. Beautifully executed figures of gods and priests, mythological animals and various objects are carved on these seals, and Ready's contribution was to provide a fine flat surface showing all the details, instead of having to study them in the round.

Perhaps his greatest success lies in the restoration of the Gates of Shalamaneser which are still on view in the Museum. The bronze plates when discovered were badly oxydized and broken into hundreds of fragments, but Ready and his two sons, Talbot and Augustus, set to work and brought them back into the condition in which they are to be seen today.

Having given pride of place to Rawlinson, the 'Father of Assyriology, mention must certainly be made of several other British Assyriologists, and perhaps the most notable of these was the

Rev. Archibald Sayce, DD. He was a noted lecturer, who, it was said, by his clear and lucid expositions 'made the dry bones of Assyriology come to life'.

He published many books, and was also a decipherer of the Wan Inscriptions and the Old Susian texts of Mal-Amir. As a cleric, he adapted his findings to the better understanding of the Bible.

He spared neither his time, money nor health in his researches, and was popular with the native people as he copied his inscriptions in the rocky deserts. Other civilisations and cults claimed his interest, for example those of Guinea, Java and Polynesia; in Japan he discussed Buddhism and the introduction of Christianity into China by the Nestorians.

Another cleric, the Rev C.J. Ball, MA, a noted Hebrew scholar, studied Assyrian in the light of his knowledge of Hebrew texts and became obsessed by the idea that Sumerian was related to ancient Chinese both in sound and meaning. He wrote many papers on the subject and published a book *Chinese and Sumerian* in 1913. He was a very earnest man and had a wide knowledge of archaic Chinese characters, but the test came when he endeavoured to read a tablet inscribed only in Sumerian; the result was failure, because the two languages have nothing in common.

Stephen Langdon, Professor of Assyriology, and an American who became a British subject in 1913, did Spartan work in the Sumerian language, and was the first to publish a worthwhile grammar. In the 1920s he directed several excavations at Kish and published many volumes on the results of his work there.

G.R. Driver, MA, MC, one-time Fellow and Librarian of Magdalen College, Oxford, contributed a great many learned articles on Assyrian, Hebrew and Aramaic subjects, and for the reader who may wish to delve more deeply into the present subject, Driver's name should be remembered.

In America, the 'Father of Assyriology' was Professor David Gordon Lyon, who was born in 1852 in Alabama. He was among the first Americans to become enamoured of Assyriology, and

studied in Germany under Delitzsch at Leipzig. His first published work was an edition of an inscription of Sargon II (722-
705 BC), which he followed with an *Assyrian Manual.* This was
found to be a clear and useful introduction for students interested in the Assyrian language.

At about this time (1833), the Americans thought that their
involvement in the rush for Mesopotamian antiquities was long
overdue and, as a result, some of the Universities sent out teams
to the area. As the French and British had pretty well cleaned
up in Assyria, the Americans turned their attentions to Babylonia. Here, they were very fortunate, for they unearthed tens
of thousands of tablets of every description as well as other
kinds of antiquities, which found their way to American
museums.

American Assyriologists owe a debt of gratitude to a man
named J.H. Haynes, who was the photographer attached to one
of the expeditions; he was neither an Assyriologist nor an expert
archaeologist but through his devotion to the work being carried
on at Niffar, he was responsible for acquiring over fifty thousand
tablets and other objects for the University of Pennsylvania.

Naturally the British, French, and Americans were not the
only people to have their interest awakened by the then new
science of Assyriology; the Germans, with their characteristic
determination and application did splendid work, among them
being the aforementioned Professor Delitzsch, Professor Dr.
Eberhard Schrader, Professor Dr. Fritz Hommel, and Professor
Dr. Carl Bezold. Other tireless workers were Lehmann-Haupt,
Winckler, Sachau, Weissbach, Ebeling, and the Rev. Dr. John
Strassmaier.

Scandinavian and Dutch Assyriologists contributed important
translations, though not on such a scale as the British and Germans, while in Italy there were quite a few names to be reckoned
with: scholars such as Bruto Teloni, Antonius Deimel, Enrico
Besta, Biagio Bruci and Giustino Boson.

Although scholars the world over were being constantly

thrilled by new 'finds', fresh translations and the like, Assyriology failed to capture the interest of the general public; it was only when translations from the monuments began to make the Bible live for them that they sat up and took notice, eagerly reading every popular book on the subject and clamouring for more. But people like Rawlinson and Hincks who really knew their subject, were far too busy working on their cuneiform texts to be able to spare the time to write popular articles and books, which was a great pity, because much of the material published in the popular journals of the time had been written by enthusiastic journalists without basic training in Assyriology.

Chapter 12

Just as in ancient Egypt, the schoolboys of Babylon and Assyria had their problems in trying to learn the 'Three Rs', except that their writing material was clay and their pen the stylus.

The profession of scribe was a highly favoured one, and regular schools were attached to the temples, but if the parents wished, a boy could be set to work under a private teacher. As in the case of the scribes in Egypt, or the artists in Rembrandt's time, a master would be pleased to take under his protection bright boys as apprentices who were keen to enter the profession.

As well as learning the art of writing in the master's home, boys would accompany him as he went about his duties, thereby not only learning how to write, but how to use words and to learn at first hand how business was conducted.

'Textbooks' and trial clay tablets by the hundred have been recovered in archaeological digs; on the latter, the fine writing of the teacher is on the left-hand side, while on the right can be seen the pupils' efforts to copy it. The room used for teaching was most likely furnished with a wooden box filled with fine pure clay; when a boy wanted a tablet, he went to the box, took a small handful, made a ball and flattened it out. It now resembled a thick lens, and the surface was ready for writing upon.

Tablets have been found which have been cut in half, bearing incredibly neat writing; these are probably teachers' models which were given to pupils to copy. Many of these copies have come down to us, some of them well-written, but others so bad that modern decipherers could make nothing of them. Pupils' mistakes consisted of characters lacking certain essential strokes, crowding characters together so badly that the strokes of one 'word' got mixed with the next, and rows of characters written badly out of line.

It seems that the Sumerians, the Assyrians and the Babylonians were excellent mathematicians. Like other ancient peoples, they used the decimal system, which has its origin in counting on the fingers; they also employed another system in which the unit was not ten but sixty. Although it is plain that the decimal system permits division only by 2, 5, and 10, if other numbers are used, we are left with a recurring decimal or an awkward fraction, it appears (although I am no expert) that 60 can be divided evenly by 2, 3, 4, 5, 6, 10, 12, 15, and even further. It seems to me that this was extremely brilliant of those ancient peoples, because it had greater adaptability than the ordinary decimal system. Moreover, the remains of this system is still with us — the hour and the minute are both divided into sixty parts, while the circle contains 360 degrees. Regarding the decimal system, I suppose that if we had been born with six fingers, everybody from the earliest days would have counted in dozens!

The science of geometry was known to the Babylonians; in the Assyrian Galleries in the British Museum there are some examples of geometric problems inscribed on clay tablets. Upon them, squares of given dimensions are sub-divided into various figures and the students were required to calculate the areas.

As for geography, the Babylonian schoolboy had little to learn; he was taught that the earth was quite flat, though possessing certain mountainous features, and that the sky was a great dome. Outside this area there was some vague idea of a boundless ocean, while somewhere on the earth there was a mysterious mountain wherein the gods dwelt. All the ancient peoples had similar notions about the shape of the earth, and to them, the idea must have appeared perfectly logical. As the reader well knows, it was not until a very late period in human history that the concept of the earth as a globe was accepted.

Another race of people, the Aztecs, who were the Indian inhabitants of South America also used an unusual numerical system. They counted, not in tens or sixties, but in twenties. The writing of the Aztecs was pictographic and various signs, unrelated to each other, formed words, names, titles, etc., very much after the style of our Egyptian hieroglyphics. They had no alphabet; if they wanted to indicate the town of Pantepec, for example, the priest-scribe would make a little drawing of a flag, *pantli*, sprouting out of a hill, *tepec*. If they had had a town called Oxford, they would have drawn an ox over some rippling lines; many of you will recall that the firm making Morris cars used this device several years ago.

Aztec pictographs never developed into a written language, therefore it was not possible to employ the signs for expressing ideas, writing a letter or a description of anything. Quantities, however, could be indicated by a system of standard signs; for low numbers up to twenty they drew the required number of dots, or in the case of 2 or 3, they would draw two or three finger-tips; 20 was represented by a little flag, and they would use multiples of flags until 380 was reached. After this, a little drawing suggestive of a fern frond indicated the number 400.

The next and final unit (20x20x20)=8,000, was indicated by a pictograph of a leather bag. Now, all the priest-scribe had to do if he wanted to show on a sheet of paper '1,242 blankets' was to draw a folded blanket, and from the top would sprout three ferns, two flags, and two fingers. A hundred jars of honey would show a netted honey jar with handles and from a stem above it would be drawn five flags.

It may be asked, if the 'writing' of the Aztecs was so primitive and incapable of being used for normal communications, how is it that we are in possession of so many of their historical events?

Briefly, the answer is this: after the Spanish Conquest of the Aztec people, their history was set down by Spanish historians who listened to the chanters reciting their folk-tales and sagas, and to the priests, whose memories for important events in the nation's history would be more reliable.

In brief then, the Aztecs and allied peoples relied upon memory and the *spoken* word, rather than upon an organised system of writing, although a sort of paper was manufactured from the bark of a certain tree.

The earliest examples of Chinese calligraphy are to be seen in the British Museum, and date from about 1100 BC. These examples are in the form of divination texts scratched upon pieces of bone, but it is only reasonable to assume that somewhere, as yet undiscovered, there must be many more pieces of bone or metal far older than the exhibits in the Museum.

At no stage was the writing of China entirely undecipherable; over the centuries, it developed as a living language, but so vast is the country that the written and spoken word varied so much, (and still does) that a citizen from one state could not read the script nor understand the dialect of the next.

An attempt to remedy this state of affairs was made by Li Ssu, the Prime Minister under the notorious Emperor Ch'in Shih Huang Ti who built the Great Wall of China (200 BC). A new official script was produced by one of Li Ssu's ministries, and the writing used in China at the present time is derived from those reforms carried out some two hundred years before the Christian era.

And what of today? The reform of the Chinese language is once again being pushed into the forefront of urgent affairs. Chinese newspapers are urging the need for greater simplification of the Chineses characters, or failing that, full Romanisation, that is to say, to have the Chinese language printed in Roman letters.

Needless to say, the latter move is, and always will be strenuously resisted because of the ingrained habits of three thousand years. Nevertheless, some progress is being made in reducing the number of strokes in a great number of characters. For example, there are some characters needing as many as thirty-two strokes

DEVELOPMENT OF THE ALPHABET

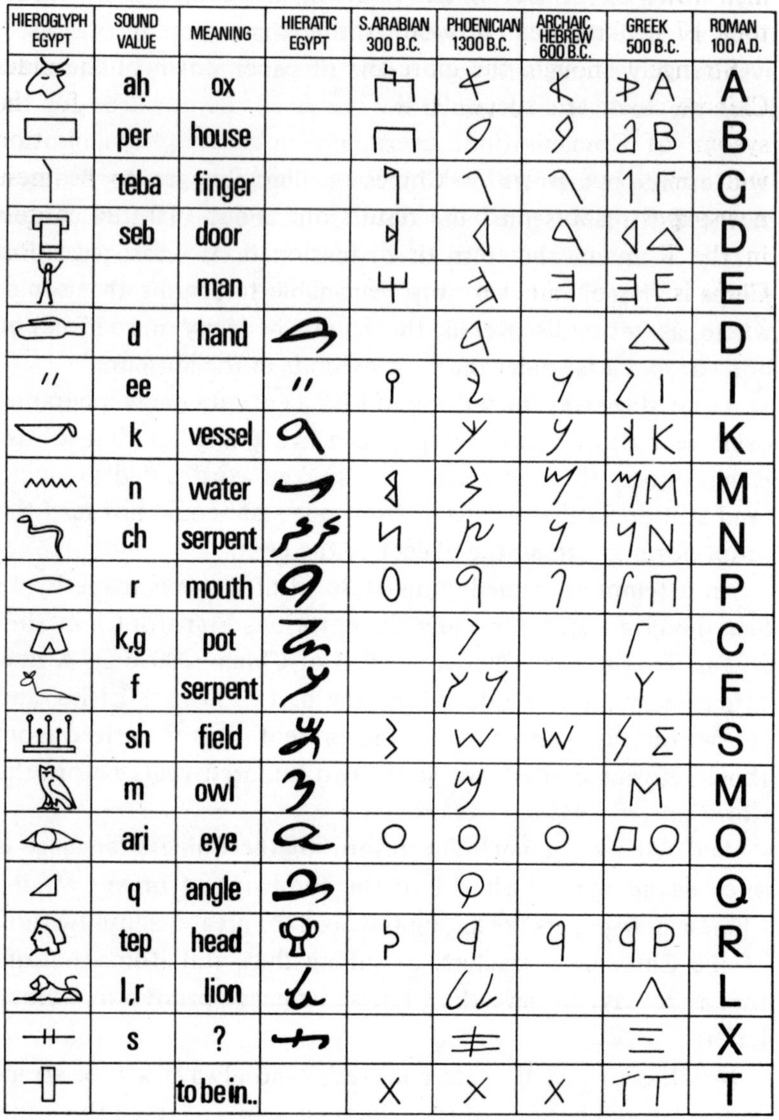

HIEROGLYPH EGYPT	SOUND VALUE	MEANING	HIERATIC EGYPT	S. ARABIAN 300 B.C.	PHOENICIAN 1300 B.C.	ARCHAIC HEBREW 600 B.C.	GREEK 500 B.C.	ROMAN 100 A.D.
🐂	aḥ	ox	⼘	⼎	⼆	⼂A	A
⬜	per	house		⼍	⼄	⼄	⼂B	B
⼁	teba	finger	⼄	⼀	⼀	1⼁	G
⼗	seb	door	⼘	⼂	△	⼂△	D
⼈		man	⼖	⼂	⼂	⼂E	E
⼎	d	hand	⼂		⼂	△	D
ʺ	ee		ʺ	⼁	⼂	⼂	⼂Ⅰ	I
⼂	k	vessel	⼂		⼘	⼘	⼘K	K
⼂	n	water	⼂	⼂	⼂	⼘	⼘M	M
⼂	ch	serpent	⼂	⼘	⼘	⼘	⼘N	N
⼂	r	mouth	⼂	0	⼂	⼂	⼂⼍	P
⼂	k,g	pot	⼂		⼂		⼁	C
⼂	f	serpent	⼂		⼘⼘		Y	F
⼂	sh	field	⼂	⼂	w	W	⼂Σ	S
⼂	m	owl	⼂		⼘		M	M
⼂	ari	eye	⼂	0	0	0	�口O	O
⼂	q	angle	⼂		⼂			Q
⼂	tep	head	⼂	⼂	⼂	⼂	⼂P	R
⼂	l,r	lion	⼂		⼘⼘		⼂	L
⼬	s	?	⼂		⼂		⼂	X
⼬		to be in..		X	X	X	⼂T	T

to form the required ideogram; in one case, this has been slimmed down to six. Before the reforms, the ideogram for 'turtle' took 17 strokes; it can now be written in seven.

Strangely enough, the more the slimming down of the older Chinese characters succeeds, the less need there will be for the system of Romanisation. Eventually, I believe, Romanisation will come, but it will take a long, long time before Chinese newspaper readers read the results of the local fan-tan contest in the Roman characters that are printed on this page. But China is very old and very wise, and she can afford to wait.

Index

132